two-hour beaded projects

more than 200 designs

two-hour beaded projects

more than 200 designs

ann
benson

Sterling Publishing Co., Inc. New York
A Sterling / Chapelle Book

CHAPELLE:

Jo Packham, Owner
Cathy Sexton, Editor
Staff: Malissa Boatwright, Sara Casperson, Rebecca Christensen, Kellie Cracas,
Amber Hansen, Holly Hollingsworth, Susan Jorgensen, Susan Laws,
Amanda McPeck, Barbara Milburn, Leslie Ridenour, Cindy Rooks,
Cindy Stoeckl, Ryanne Webster, and Nancy Whitley

HAZEN PHOTOGRAPHY:

Kevin Dilley, Photographer
Cherie Herrick, Photo Stylist

MODELS:

Amy Broadbent and Sara Buehler

If you have any questions or comments or would like information on specialty products featured in this book, please contact: Chapelle, Ltd., Inc., P.O. Box 9252, Ogden, UT 84409 • (801) 621-2777 • (801) 621-2788 Fax

Library of Congress Cataloging-in-Publication Data

Benson, Ann.
        Two-hour beaded projects : more than 200 designs / by Ann Benson.
                p.   cm.
        "A Sterling / Chapelle book."
        Includes index.
        ISBN 0-8069-4270-3
        1. Beadwork.   2. Jewelry making.   3. House furnishings.
        I. Title
        TT860.B487   1995
        745.58'2--dc20   95-37042
                                                          CIP

10 9 8 7 6 5 4 3 2 1

Published by Sterling Publishing Company, Inc.
387 Park Avenue South, New York, NY 10016
© 1996 by Chapelle Ltd.
Distributed in Canada by Sterling Publishing
c/o Canadian Manda Group, One Atlantic Avenue, Suite 105
Toronto, Ontario, Canada M6K 3E7
Distributed in Great Britain and Europe by Cassell PLC
Wellington House, 125 Strand, London WC2R 0BB, England
Distributed in Australia by Capricorn Link (Australia) Pty Ltd.
P.O. Box 6651, Baulkham Hills, Business Centre, NSW 2153, Australia
Printed in Hong Kong
All Rights Reserved

Sterling ISBN 0-8069-4270-3

about the author ...

Ann Benson is a well-known designer and author. This is her fourth book of bead designs. Her work for international corporations includes toys, games, and children's craft kits.

In her leisure time, Ann enjoys bicycling and cross-country skiing, and she is currently working on her second novel.

Ann and her family reside in Amherst, Massachusetts.

Miss Benson dedicates this book to her mom and dad.

contents ...

About the author 8
Bead shapes 9
A little about beads 10
Tools 12
Bead sizes 12
Beading components 13
Findings & components 14
General instructions 16

chapter one jewelry

Random twist necklaces 21
Amber & cloisonne necklace 23
Turquoise tube necklace 24
Lucky elephant necklace 24
Turquoise drum necklace 24
Crystal necklaces 26
Chevron necklace 28
Lavender matte necklace 30
Coil necklace 31
Triple rainbow necklace 31
Beaded strawberry necklace 32
Beaded pear necklace 32
Blue on blue necklace 33
Porcelain rose necklace 34
Embellished lace necklace 35
Striped clay necklace & earrings 36
Green yipes stripes necklace,
    bracelet & earrings 37

Lilac tassel necklace & earrings 38
Indian agate necklace & earrings 39
Yin-yang necklace, bracelet & earrings 40
Jingle bells necklace & earrings 41
Pearl spray earrings 42
Turquoise drop earrings 42
Amethyst cabochon earrings 43
Zuni bear earrings 43
Silver heart earrings 44
Turquoise cabochon earrings 44
Sun-star earrings 45
Sand dollar earrings 45
French wire earrings 46
Polymer clay earrings 47
Hex earrings 48
Component earrings 50
Artistic dangle earrings 52
Ear cuffs 54
Braided bracelets 55
White disk bracelet 56
Button bracelet 56
Peruvian bracelet 56
Expansion bracelet 57
Multi-bracelet bracelet 57
Cabochon bracelets 58
Silver & amethyst cabochon watch 59
Liquid silver bracelet 60
Twisted bracelet 60
Anklets 61
Floral oval pin 62
Petite paisley pin 62
Oval flower pin 62
Cosmic leather pin 64
Amber & jade pin 64
Dangle charm pin 65
Petit flower pins 66
Stick pins 68
Rosary beads 69

chapter
two
hair

Bargello barrette 71
Blue diamond barrette 72
Purple diamond barrette 73
Floral barrette 74
Tortoise shell barrette 75
Velvet rose ribbon barrette 75
Celtic weave combs 76
Clinch combs 77
Beaded hairsticks 78
Dangle hairsticks 79

chapter
three
wearables

Pearl & lace collar 81
Black lace collar 82
Frosted amber pocket embellishment 83
Simple garment embellishments 84
Beaded collar & pockets 86
Blazer cuffs & pocket 87
Coin dress 88
Gloves 89
Multi-color button covers 90
Flat disk button covers 91

chapter
four
decor

Jeweled heart boxes 93
Perfume bottles 94
Charm bottles 95
House magnet 96
Stationery boxes 97
Jade tree in clay pot 98
Frames 100
Vase 102
Votive cups 103
Suncatchers 104
Napkin rings 106
Candles 107
Crystal-drop candelabra 108
Sachet box, bag & pillow 109
Candle shades 110
Beaded vanity set 112
Flower vase 113
Icicles 113
Drawer knobs 114
Decorative eggs 116
Heart ornament 117
Wooden tray 118
Safety-pin basket 119
Victorian ornaments 120
Hanging wooden ornaments 121
Embellished canning jar 122
Metal pot stand 123
Bronze candlestick collar 124
Crystal candlestick skirt 125
Gourd ornament.. 126

Metric conversions 127
Index 128

introduction ...

The history of traditional jewelry and its decoration began with the pieces worn by hunters and gatherers in their caves. It spans thousands of years and not only connects every continent, but every civilization of the world.

The story begins with necklaces that were made from the bone and teeth of animals and from the flowers and fruits that were gathered. It progresses through the ages to the gold, silver, and precious stones that were used to make the collars, crowns, and goblets for kings and noblemen.

There is a tale, told during these same years, that is of decorative objects and jewelry made and worn for folk and ethnic costumes and for decorating the homes of the more common people and tribesmen.

These pieces were ornaments whose makers had no rules or customs, whose style was dictated by the time, the event, the place, and the artist.

The making and wearing of jewelry and special objects that are adorned by jewels has always been prompted by vanity, status, religion, and superstition. They have been used throughout time for trading, for the expression of love, and for the giving of gifts. These pieces that are so admired and so sought after have sometimes been extravagantly ornate and sometimes priceless, yet have sometimes been made of the simplest of materials and in the shortest amount of time. Descendants of the latter are the pieces that are presented here. Those pieces that are much admired and constantly worn or displayed by the receiver yet inexpensive and quickly made by the giver.

Here in TWO-HOUR BEADED PROJECTS, not only can traditional pieces of jewelry such as necklaces, bracelets, and earrings be found, but unique styles have been created to suit many personalities. Hair accessories have been included as have many ideas for embellishing wearables. There are also ideas for creating home decorative accessories, such as adorning candle holders, glass vases, stationery boxes, suncatchers, decorative bottles, and much more.

Here are pieces that can be made for a daughter, a mother, or a friend. Here are pieces that are perfect for gift giving or for keeping for oneself. Here are pieces that are beautiful in their simplicity and practical in their monetary value.

It is hoped that what is within these pages will give hours of enjoyment not only in the making, but in the giving and receiving.

bead shapes ...

bugle beads

Bugle beads are essentially very long seed beads. They are long thin tubes which come in a variety of lengths. Bugle beads are available in many finishes, but the color selection is limited. Some bugle beads are twisted in the manufacturing process.

faceted beads

Faceted beads are often referred to as "crystals." They are made in many different shapes and colors.

Faceted beads are classified as molded crystal and cut crystal. Cut crystal is more expensive and comes in a wider range of shapes than molded crystal.

Finishes can be applied to any faceted bead. Molded crystal beads are available with metallic finishes — usually in silver or bronze.

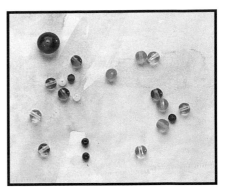

round beads

Round beads, of course, are spherical. They come in many sizes and are measured in millimeters. They can be found in numerous colors and finishes and can be made from polymer clay.

cabochons

Cabochons are flattened beads without holes and are usually mounted in a bezel cup (refer to page 13). They are available in a wide range of sizes and can be made from almost any material, including polymer clay. There is a good selection of cabochons available in semiprecious stones.

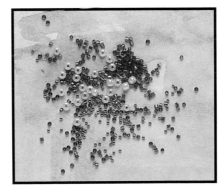

seed beads

Seed beads are small glass beads and are the most common type of bead used. They are available with many finishes and are made in many, many colors. They come in a variety of sizes — the larger the number, the smaller the bead.

fancy shaped beads

Fancy shaped beads can vary from cylindrical, cube, and oval to twisted disks and tubes, triangles and tear drops, lozenges, and donuts. Many of these beads make great centerpieces on all varieties of jewelry.

a little about beads ...

glass beads

Glass beads are available in an unbelievable range of size, shape, and color. It is no wonder glass beads are used more often than any other type of decorative bead.

Glass beads can be molded or hand-blown. Molded glass beads can be made in almost any color of glass and are readily available in any bead store. Hand-blown glass beads can be exquisitely beautiful.

plastic beads

Some of the most exciting beads available are plastic beads. Plastic beads can be pale and translucent or wildly colorful, and their variation is nearly endless. Because they are almost always molded, the holes in the beads are uniform in size.

Besides affordability, plastic beads offer many advantages to the serious beadworker. Plastic beads are lightweight and consistently strong. This makes plastic beads an ideal candidate for use on heavier-weight cords and multiple strand cords.

metal beads

The price of metal beads is largely determined by their precious metal content. Sterling silver, gold-filled, and gold-plated beads can be costly.

There are, however, several styles and sizes of metal beads that are available in surface-washed base metal beads. These beads are readily available, lightweight, and inexpensive.

natural beads

Natural beads include wood, stone, and bone beads. These beads have a special beauty.

Wood beads are lightweight, relatively inexpensive, and widely available. Many varieties of wood are used to make wood beads, and each is unique because of its grain and finish. Unlacquered wood beads can be soaked in vanilla or fragrant oils and worn as perfume.

Stone beads are very popular and include turquoise, pearls, and semiprecious stones. Because the are derived from nature, they are available in a myriad of sizes, shapes, and colors.

Bone beads are made from bone or tusk. These beads are often made into disks, which are usually side-drilled for use in making jewelry pieces.

ceramic beads

Ceramic beads can be either rough or decorated. Both beads are made from the same materials; however, the differences lie in the way the surfaces are treated.

Rough ceramic beads can be glazed, but because of the rough, grainy surface after firing the beads, they appear to be unglazed.

Decorated ceramic beads are often glazed before firing, but some decorated ceramic beads are painted with permanent colors after firing. Decals are often added to the surface of the fired ceramic bead.

Most ceramic beads tend to have a soft, natural color, but some varieties have dye added to the clay before the beads are formed. Therefore, colors are literally unrestricted.

Ceramic beads come in an unlimited variety of shapes and sizes but can be quite heavy.

clay beads

Polymer clays are used to make clay beads. Truly a modern wonder, polymer clay allows any bead to be made at any time in any shape, any size, and any color!

There are many fine instructional manuals on the subject of making clay beads.

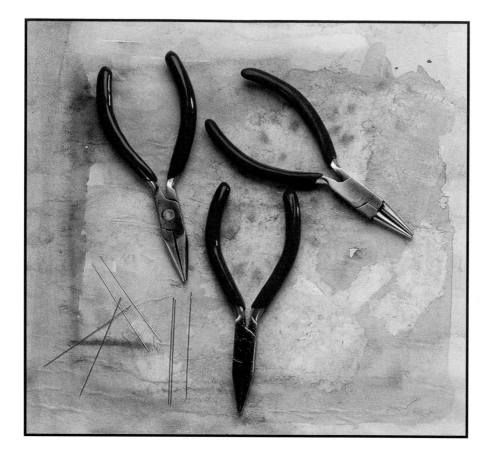

tools ...

Very few tools are required for successful beadwork. A good assortment of needles and sharp scissors are essential.

Wirecutters, round-nose pliers, and needle-nose pliers are necessary for making jewelry with headpins and eyepins.

bead sizes ...

Round beads: 4mm, 6mm, 8mm, 10mm, 12mm

Oval cabochons: 4x6mm, 5x7mm, 6x8mm, 8x10mm, 10x12mm, 10x14mm, 13x18mm, 18x25mm

Round cabochons: 25mm, 20mm, 16mm, 12mm, 10mm, 8mm, 6mm, 5mm, 4mm, 3mm

Seed Beads:
6/0 seed beads
8/0 seed beads
11/0 seed beads
14/0 seed beads
12/0 three cuts
hex beads

Bugle Beads:
20mm bugle beads
15mm bugle beads
#5 bugle beads
#3 bugle beads
#2 bugle beads

Photos are actual size.

beading components ...

pre-strung beads

Pre-strung beads are available in a number of different varieties, sizes, and colors.

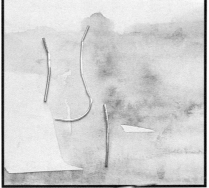

french wire

French wire is a tightly wound coil of very fine metal wire. It is available in a variety of diameters and finishes, and is extremely flexible. It can be cut with ordinary scissors without marring the cutting surface.

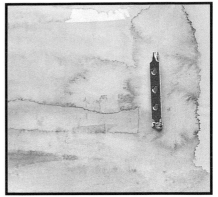

pin backs

Pin backs are available in a wide range of styles and sizes. They can be made from gold- and silver-plated metal.

Pin backs are generally glued to the back of the pin.

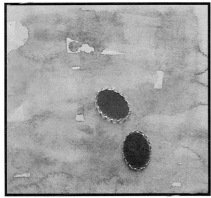

bezel cups

Bezel cups hold flat-backed cabochons and can easily be incorporated into simple jewelry designs. They are available in a variety of sizes.

The outer wall of the cup is a series of loops, which give it a lacy appearance. These loops can be bent and used as joining loops quite easily. The remainder of the loops can be bent inward in close contact with the cabochon to hold it in the cup, or a tiny dot of glue can be placed in the center of the cup to hold the stone in place.

ear findings

Ear findings are available in a wide range of styles and sizes. They can be made from plated base metal or genuine gold and silver.

Ear findings include French ear wires, ear clips, and ear posts. Ear clips or posts can be glued to the back of the earring or to a bead. Ear wires usually come with a loop in order to hang an intended finding.

Niobium is a finish that is often used to enhance the look of a pair of earrings and can be found in a variety of bright colors.

button cover blanks

Button cover blanks are made from base metal and can be found in a brass- or silver-colored finish. The size is usually about 3/4" in diameter, and will accommodate buttons up to a slightly larger size.

findings & components ...

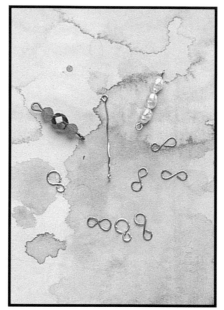

headpins & eyepins

Headpins and eyepins come in a variety of gauges, finishes, and lengths.

Headpins look much like nails with one flat end. This flat end keeps beads from falling off the pin.

Eyepins are used in the same manner as headpins, but they have a loop instead of a flat end. Eyepins are often used to make figure-eight connectors.

figure-eight & beaded connectors

Figure-eight connectors are small links in the shape of the number "8" which can be made from an eyepin or from metal wire.

Beaded connectors are extended figure-eight connectors that have beads in between the loops on the ends. Beaded connectors can also be made from headpins.

clasps

Clasps can be very ornate or very simple and they can act as part of the design. They come in a variety of finishes and shapes, but they must be coordinated with the beadwork.

It is recommended that barrel clasps not be used when assembling bracelets — they must be closed using both hands!

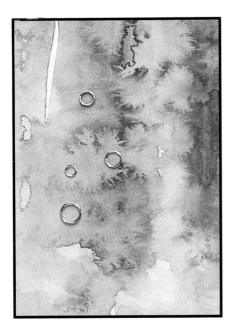

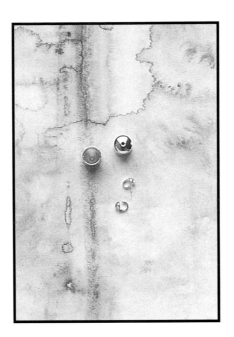

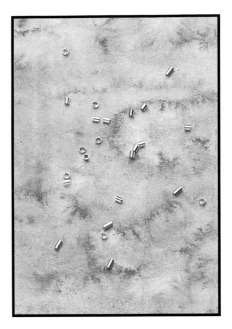

rings

Rings are used to join components, such as clasps or strung beads. They are available in a wide range of sizes and finishes.

Jump rings have a gap in the circle and separate easily with pliers.

Split rings are tiny key holders — the ring is doubled onto itself for better surety.

Unless crimps are used, rings are generally used when attaching clasps.

end caps & end cups

End caps can be found in cylindrical and conical shapes and in a variety of metal finishes. They are used to create a finished look on the ends of multi-strand necklaces, bracelets, and earrings.

End cups hold the knot of beading thread and are then attached to the clasp and jump ring on necklaces and bracelets. They come in silver-tone and gold-tone finishes.

crimps

Crimps are flattened over wire or leather with the use of pliers to secure a strand of beads to a clasp or other finding. It is important that the crimp being used is the proper size for the material being secured.

When possible, coordinate the finish of the crimp with the finish of the clasp.

general instructions ...

adding a new length of thread

When about three inches of thread remains unbeaded on the needle, it is time to add a new thread.

Remove the needle from the old thread and cut a new 30" length. Thread the needle so that a 5" tail remains. A longer thread tends to tangle, and a shorter thread necessitates frequent rethreadings.

Tie a square knot so that the knot lands about 1" from where the old thread emerges from the beadwork. Refer to the diagrams below.

Place a tiny dot of glue on the knot. Wipe off any excess glue, but the glue need not be dry before proceeding.

Continue beading as if one continuous thread were being used. Let the thread ends protrude from the work until the new thread is well established within the weave. Refer to the diagrams below. Pull gently on the ends and clip them close so that they disappear into the weave. It might be necessary to use a smaller needle until the area of the knot has been passed.

assembling beaded connectors

A beaded connector is an extended figure-eight connector with a bead(s) added in the middle. It can also be referred to when threading a bead(s) onto a headpin.

When starting with an eyepin, trim it to 3/8" beyond the last bead. Using round-nose pliers, form a second loop in the opposite direction as shown in the diagram below. Many eyepins can be beaded and joined together to form a necklace or bracelet. When working with metal wire, form the first loop, trim to 3/8", and form the second loop. Any wire used to make a connector should be substantial enough to retain the shape of the loops. If the wire can easily be shaped, it is probably not strong enough for use as a jewelry connector.

When starting with a headpin, simply thread on the beads and cut the headpin with wirecutters so there is 1/4" to 3/8" excess. Using round-nose pliers, form a loop in the top of the headpin as shown in the diagram below, then close it around the intended finding. Headpins are the most commonly used finding when assembling earrings. A headpin with beads can be attached to an eyepin and will dangle with a nice movement.

attaching clasps

Clasps have loops by which they may be attached. Depending on the type of material used for stringing, they may be attached to end caps or joined to the strand by crimping.

End caps are sometimes used to join multiple strands to a clasp. Some clasps have multiple loops and are designed for a specific number of strands, in which case you should attach the strand directly to the clasp loops using end caps or crimps to secure the fiber.

attaching end caps

Cover a final knot, holding several strands together, with cylindrical or conical end caps.

Open the loop on an eyepin, and insert it through the hole in the end cap. Close the loop around the knot. Pull the knot into the cap, then trim the excess eyepin to 3/8" and form another loop, which should be attached to your clasp.

Refer to the diagrams below.

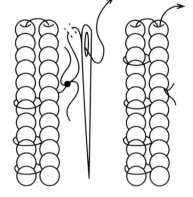

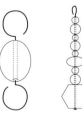

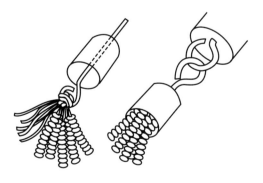

brick-stitching

Brick-stitch is a diagonal weaving technique in which the beads lay against one another like alternating bricks. All work progresses outward from a central foundation row. Each new row is looped into the previous row one bead at a time. The resulting weave is strong and flexible, and can be used for many different purposes.

The foundation row is worked with two needles. Cut a length of thread about 24" long, and thread each end onto a needle. Center the first bead of the foundation row between the two needles, then form the foundation row. Refer to the first diagram below.

Thereafter, you will work with one needle at a time. It is convenient to remove the needle from the thread end not currently in use, as it minimizes the tangling of the two threads. Refer to the diagrams below.

For rethreadings, refer to "adding a new length of thread" on page 16.

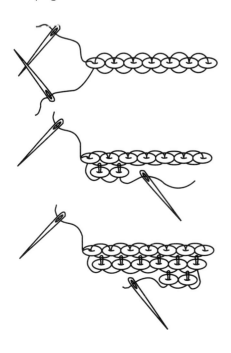

crimping

Secure tigertail or nylon to a jump ring or clasp, using a crimp which is squeezed tightly with pliers over the trimmed end to form a strong loop.

Refer to the diagrams below.

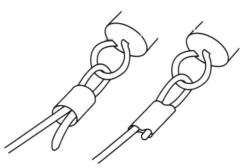

embellishing simple objects

Many simple pieces of jewelry can be dramatized with the simple addition of drops or hangers.

When planning to embellish jewelry, choose jewelry pieces that have openings suitable for inserting loops.

To make sure the drops or hangers move freely, make the loops a bit larger. When trimming the headpins, leave an excess of 1/2" instead of the usual 3/8".

finishing strands

The diagrams below show two methods used for finishing strands of beads that have been strung on sewing thread or beading cord.

Finish the knotted strands with one large knot — knotted over itself until it is of substantial size. With matching sewing thread, sew the knot to an attractive clasp (ring shown) or knot nylon thread into an end cup, then attach it with a jump ring to a clasp.

fusing fabric

To fuse fabric to beadwork, a thick white towel, completed beadwork, fusible webbing, fabric, a sheet of white paper, and an iron are needed.

Layer and center the components in the following manner, starting at the bottom: the towel, the beadwork face down, the fusible webbing with paper removed, the fabric right side up, and the sheet of white paper.

Press the iron down flat for five seconds. Shift the iron and press for two more seconds to eliminate any steam holes. Allow the piece to cool completely. With nail scissors, trim the excess from around the beadwork. Run a thin line of diluted white glue around the entire trimmed edge to secure.

needle-weaving

The work in needle-weaving always proceeds in the direction of the beadworker's dominant hand.

To begin, make a "stopper bead," which keeps the design pattern beads from slipping off the needle. Refer to the diagrams below. Cut a length of thread about 30 inches long and thread a needle so that a 5" tail remains.

Slip one bead over the needle and position it about 3 inches from the long end of the thread. Loop the thread back through the bead and pull it tightly. Secure the stopper bead to a flat or slightly curved surface to stabilize the thread. Remove the stopper bead after the first few rows.

Thread the beads of row 1 from top to bottom. Refer to the diagrams below. Skip the last bead threaded, inserting the needle back through all the beads on the thread. The needle should emerge from the top bead of row 1.

Thread the beads of row 2, again reading from top to bottom. Refer to the diagrams below.

Insert the needle into the loop exposed at the bottom of row 1. Pull the thread gently until the whole second row is taut, but not tight. It should rest against the first row without much puckering.

Insert the needle into the last bead of row 2, and bring the thread out until it is taut, but not tight. Loop the thread around row 1 so that it nestles in the space between beads 12 and 11 of row 2, bringing the needle out in the space between beads 10 and 9 on row 2. Again, the thread should be taut, but not tight.

Loop the thread around row 1 so that it nestles in the space between beads 10 and 9 of row 1. Insert the needle into the next three beads on row 2 — beads 9, 8, and 7 — and bring the needle out in the space between beads 7 and 6 on row 2.

Tighten the thread again, then loop it around the first row so that it nestles in the space between beads 7 and 6 on row 1. Insert the needle into the next three beads on row 2 — beads 6, 5, and 4 — and repeat the looping and inserting process until the thread emerges from bead 1 of row 2. After row 2, the work may no longer need to be stabilized. It gets easier and easier to handle as the weaving grows.

For rethreadings, refer to "adding a new length of thread" on page 16.

surface beading

Surface beading requires beads to be sewn on individually and may be done on any material through which a beading needle can pass (fabric, soft leather, paper, or card stock). The method used to make the stitch is largely determined by the type of bead being sewn.

Seed Beads:

Seed beads can be sewn on singly or in multiples. For tight curves and small areas, single beading is best. For larger areas or lines, two or more beads can be sewn on at one time.

The diagram below shows two excellent methods for sewing on a single seed bead.

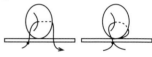

The diagram below shows how to sew on two seed beads at one time.

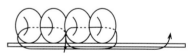

The diagram below shows how to backtrack a line of seed beads to stabilize them.

The diagram below shows a long row of seed beads being held in place by couching stitches.

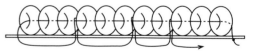

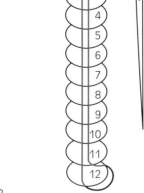

Row 1

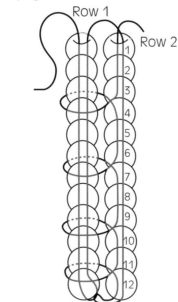

Row 1   Row 2

Odd-Shaped Beads:

The method used to sew on these beads is largely determined by the shape of the bead.

Bugle beads, pearls, round beads, flat beads, and other odd-shaped beads can be sewn on using some of the techniques diagrammed below.

Note that in some cases the larger bead is anchored to the surface using a seed bead.

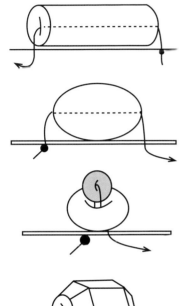

working with leather cord

Using leather cord as a foundation for the piece of jewelry makes the project extremely simple. The most important thing to keep in mind is that the beads chosen must have a large enough hole to accommodate the bulkiness of the leather cord.

Wood, bone, and metal beads tend to have larger holes than glass beads, and beads can always be made from polymer clay with custom-sized holes.

Cut the leather cord in the length needed. Then, simply thread the desired beads onto the cord and crimp on both trimmed ends.

Open the loops on the clasp, and close them around the crimp loops.

If necessary, refer to the diagrams below.

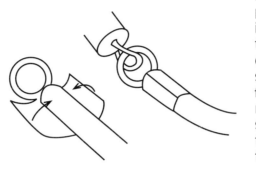

working with polymer clay

Working with clay:

Work the clay in your hands until it is soft and pliable. Form the softened clay into desired shapes. A rolling pin can be used to flatten the clay, or it can be run through the flattening wheels of a pasta machine. If the pasta machine does not create the correct thickness, combine two or more layers together. The thickness of the clay should be at least 1/8" for strength and stability. Do not use a pasta machine which may later be used to make edible pasta!

Form a U-shaped piece with the headpin scrap, and insert it into the top of the shape — be sure to leave enough space to slip the hanging cord or ribbon through.

Bake on a clean cookie sheet covered with aluminum foil at 200° F for 20 minutes. Allow to cool before handling.

If desired, coat the shape with varnish or clear nail polish.

Pressing beads into clay.

Lay the seed beads out on a flat surface in a tight layer with the bead holes up or down. Make the desired shape from the polymer clay. Roll the clay shape in the beads, and press the beads tightly into the surface of the clay. Repeat until the entire surface is covered with beads, filling in with individual beads as needed to cover the entire surface. Do not press the beads too deep into the clay or they will disappear.

chapter one

jewelry

Pictured from left to right: Random Twist Necklace with Lamp Beads, Random Twist Necklace with Turquoise, Random Twist Necklace with Amber, Random Twist Necklace with Large Glass Beads.

random twist necklaces

Beading:

These necklaces are all multi-strand twists with fancy beads placed randomly on each length. The minimum number of strands for a good result is probably six, but as many as the end cap will accommodate can be used. Try to be conscious of the weight of the necklace when choosing the fancy beads. If they are extremely large, it might be a good idea to use plastic or hollow metal beads instead of solid glass beads.

Below is an illustration of the type of pattern that works well. The pre-twisted length should be at least 19" for a 16" to 17" twisted necklace.

Tie all the ends together. Attach them to the figure-eight connectors, and cover with the end caps. Attach to the clasp.

If necessary, refer to the photograph.

... with turquoise

Materials:

Seven turquoise beads
    of assorted shape and size
Fourteen 4mm bronze crystals
Enough matte-finish
    11/0 seed beads
    to make seven 19" strands
    using assorted colors
Two gold-tone end caps
Two gold-tone
    figure-eight connectors
One gold-tone spring clasp
One gold-tone split ring
Lightweight nylon bead cord,
    size 0

... with amber

Materials:

Seven amber beads
    of assorted shape and size
Fourteen gold 6/0 seed beads
Enough #2 bugle beads
    to make two 19" strands
    using assorted colors
Enough 11/0 seed beads
    to make five 19" strands
    using assorted colors
Two gold-tone end caps
Two gold-tone
    figure-eight connectors
One gold-tone spring clasp
One gold-tone split ring
Lightweight nylon bead cord,
    size 0

... with large glass beads

Materials:

Six large glass beads of
    assorted shapes,
    15 to 25mm
Twelve gold 6/0 seed beads
Enough 11/0 seed beads
    to make six 19" strands
    using assorted colors
Two gold-tone end caps
Two gold-tone
    figure-eight connectors
One gold-tone beehive clasp
Lightweight nylon bead cord,
    size 0

... with lamp beads

Materials:

Six lamp beads of assorted colors
Twelve gold 6/0 seed beads
Enough 9/0 three-cut beads
    to make six 19" strands
    using assorted colors
Two gold-tone end caps
Two gold-tone
    figure-eight connectors
One gold-tone beehive clasp
Lightweight nylon bead cord,
    size 0

▬▬▬	11/0 seed beads
○	6/0 seed beads
▭	fancy glass beads
⬭	fancy glass beads
○	fancy glass beads
──	loose ends

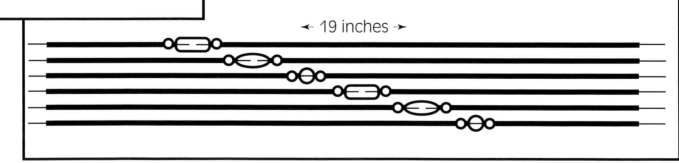

← 19 inches →

amber & cloisonne necklace

Materials:

Eight amber beads, approximately 7x11mm
Seventy medium green 11/0 seed beads
Twenty-five 8mm aventurine beads
Eighteen 8mm dark carnelian beads
Eighteen 10mm light carnelian beads
One two-sided cloisonne clasp
Fine nylon beading thread, size 0 or finer
Jewelry glue

Beading:

Using a tiny beading needle, string the beads in the pattern shown in the diagram below. Start and end with the outer aventurine bead. Insert the needle into one end of the clasp, and slide one bead over it. Insert the needle back out through the clasp hole to anchor the beads to the clasp.

Run the needle back through about two-thirds of the beads, and let the thread hang from the necklace. Thread the loose end of the nylon beading thread on the other side of the necklace, and repeat the above operation with the other side of the clasp. Run the needle back through until the two thread ends meet.

Tie the two thread ends together in a square knot, making sure to take up any slack in the necklace before doing so. Apply a small dab of glue to the knot, then bury it and the thread ends inside the adjacent beads.

If necessary, refer to the photograph.

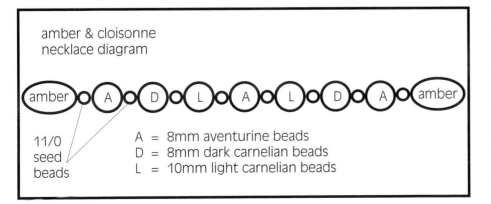

amber & cloisonne necklace diagram

amber — A — D — L — A — L — D — A — amber

11/0 seed beads

A = 8mm aventurine beads
D = 8mm dark carnelian beads
L = 10mm light carnelian beads

Pictured from left to right: Turquoise Tube Necklace, Turquoise Drum Necklace, Lucky Elephant Necklace.

turquoise tube necklace

Materials:

Fifteen 6x14mm
    turquoise tube beads
Thirty 6mm frosted
    amethyst beads
Thirty metallic blue
    11/0 seed beads
Thirty inches of
    blue niobium wire
One silver-tone barrel clasp

Beading:

Cut the niobium wire into fifteen 2-inch lengths. Following the directions for assembling beaded connectors found in the General Instructions on page 16, assemble 15 links. Form a loop on one end of each niobium wire, and thread on the beads in the following order: one 11/0 seed bead, one 6mm bead, one turquoise tube, one 6mm bead, one 11/0 seed bead. Trim to 3/8" excess, then form a new loop from the trimmed ends.

Join the loops together to form the necklace. Following the directions for attaching clasps found in the General Instructions on page 16, attach one side of the barrel clasp to each end.

If necessary, refer to the photograph.

lucky elephant necklace

Materials:

One 2" cloisonne elephant
One 3x10mm
   turquoise tube
One 12x18mm
   turquoise barrel bead
One 8x10mm
   cloisonne bead
One 4mm blue
   round glass bead
Two gold-tone end caps
One gold-tone spring clasp
One gold-tone split ring
One gold-tone headpin
Three gold-tone eyepins
Twenty-four inches of
   5mm thick woven cord
Jewelry glue

Beading:

Sew the eyepins to the ends of the woven cord, and form the loops with the trimmed eyepins. Following the directions for attaching clasps found in the General Instructions on page 16, attach the eyepins to the spring clasp. Fill the end caps with glue, and glue them to the woven cord. Thread the elephant onto the remaining eyepin, and form a loop of adequate size to reach around the woven cord, trimming the eyepin first if needed.

Following the directions for assembling beaded connectors found in the General Instructions on page 16, assemble the beaded connector in the following order from bottom to top: 4mm round glass bead, cloisonne bead, turquoise barrel bead, turquoise tube. Add the drop below the elephant.

If necessary, refer to the photograph.

turquoise drum necklace

Materials:

One 13x25mm carved
   turquoise barrel bead
Two 6mm copol rondelles
Two 14x20mm amber beads
Four 8mm
   turquoise rondelles
Six 15mm square
   frosted plastic beads
Six metallic gold
   6/0 seed beads
Three gold-tone headpins
Two gold-tone leather crimps
One gold-tone spring clasp
One gold-tone split ring
Thirty inches of metallic
   green narrow leather cord

Beading:

Follow the diagram to assemble the necklace. First, thread on the square plastic beads and tie the knots, tightening them so that they will not loosen. Leave adequate space between the knots to allow the headpins to hang freely.

Following the directions for assembling beaded connectors found in the General Instructions on page 16, assemble the three headpins and trim to 1/2" beyond the last bead.

Following the directions for working with leather cord found in the General Instructions on page 19, attach the crimps to the leather, then attach the clasp and loop to the crimps. Form a loop in the excess using round-nose pliers and close the loop around the leather.

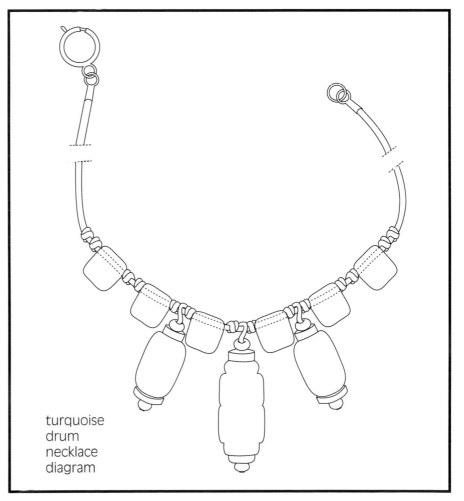

turquoise
drum
necklace
diagram

Pictured from left to right: Pastel Crystal Necklace, Bronze & Iris Crystal Necklace, Crystal Swirl Necklace.

pastel crystal necklace

Materials:

Nineteen 10mm aqua crystals
Thirty-eight 4mm green crystals
Seventy-six lavender color-lined
   11/0 seed beads
Thirty-four inches of
   green niobium wire
One silver-tone clasp

Beading:

Cut the niobium wire into nineteen equal lengths. Following the directions for assembling beaded connectors found in the General Instructions on page 16, assemble 19 links. Form a loop on one end of each wire, and thread on the beads in the following order: one 11/0 seed bead, one 4mm crystal, one 11/0 seed bead, one 10mm crystal, one 11/0 seed bead, one 4mm crystal, one 11/0 seed bead. Trim to 3/8" excess, then form a new loop from the trimmed ends.

Join the loops together to form the necklace. Following the directions for attaching clasps found in the General Instructions on page 16, attach one side of the clasp to each end.

If necessary, refer to the photograph.

bronze & iris crystal necklace

Materials:

Fourteen 8mm bronze crystals
Twenty-eight gold
  6/0 seed beads
Twenty-eight 5x7mm
  purple iris teardrops
Twenty-eight gold
  11/0 seed beads
Twenty-eight inches of
  purple niobium wire
One gold-tone barrel clasp

Beading:

Cut the niobium wire into 14 equal lengths. Following the directions for assembling beaded connectors found in the General Instructions on page 16, assemble 14 links. Form a loop on one end of each wire, and thread on the beads in the following order: one 11/0 seed bead, one teardrop, one 6/0 seed bead, one 8mm crystal, one 6/0 seed bead, one teardrop, one 11/0 seed bead. Trim to 3/8" excess, then form a new loop from the trimmed ends.

Join the loops together to form the necklace. Following the directions for attaching clasps found in the General Instructions on page 16, attach one side of the barrel clasp to each end.

If necessary, refer to the photograph.

crystal swirl necklace

Materials:

Nine 10mm
  color-swirled crystals
Sixteen 6mm
  color-swirled crystals
Six 8mm color-swirled balls
Sixty-two crystal AB
  6/0 seed beads
Thirty-two crystal AB
  11/0 seed beads
One gold-tone spring clasp
One gold-tone
Two gold-tone
  bead end cups
Nylon beading thread

Beading:

Beads of similar size can be used to create this necklace. Instead of swirled crystals, try iris crystals or aurora borealis finish crystals.

Once beads have been selected, assemble the necklace by stringing the beads following the diagram below. The diagram represents half of the necklace, starting at the center bead. Repeat the pattern on the other side.

Following the directions for attaching clasps found in the General Instructions on page 16, attach the clasp.

If necessary, refer to the photograph.

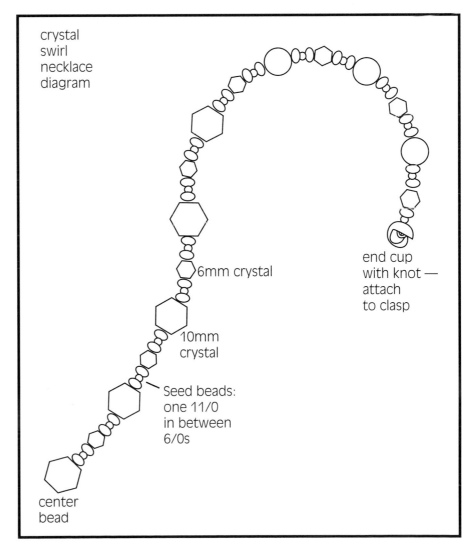

crystal
swirl
necklace
diagram

6mm crystal

10mm
crystal

Seed beads:
one 11/0
in between
6/0s

end cup
with knot —
attach
to clasp

center
bead

chevron necklace

Materials:

370 green iris 6/0 seed beads
Forty metallic silver
    6/0 seed beads
125 matte turquoise
    rainbow 6/0 seed beads
550 metallic silver
    11/0 seed beads
Thirty small turquoise chips
One gold-tone hook finding
Forty-eight inches of
    nylon beading thread,
    size 0
Fine beading needle or
    #10 quilting needle
Jewelry glue

Beading:

Assemble the foundation row. Thread the needle with the nylon beading thread. Slide one metallic silver 11/0 seed bead onto the thread; leave about 4 inches of excess, then loop back into the bead. Tighten this thread; it will be buried in the necklace later. Alternate green iris 6/0s and metallic silver 11/0s until there are 17 green iris 6/0s, then add one more metallic silver 11/0s and the hook finding. Run the needle back through all the beads on the thread, taking up the slack as you progress. Begin adding green iris and metallic silver beads, alternating the pattern as previously done, until there are a total of 104 green iris beads on the thread. Insert the needle back into the last metallic silver 11/0, then run it through the beads until the needle emerges from the 37th green iris 6/0. See the diagram on page 29 for details of the foundation row.

Add the drops as shown in the diagram on page 29, and make 30 drops. Start each drop with one metallic silver 11/0, then add the 6/0 beads in the order given, alternating with metallic silver 11/0. Refer to the diagram. End with one turquoise chip and one metallic silver 11/0. Run the thread back through all the beads on the drop, and skip to the next 11/0 on the foundation row. Run the thread through the next 6/0 on the foundation row in preparation for beginning the next drop.

Finish the thread by running it through the foundation row until it meets the original 4" tail. Tie a square knot, and dab a small amount of glue on the knot. Run the thread ends through the foundation until they are secure, then clip close.

If necessary, refer to the photograph.

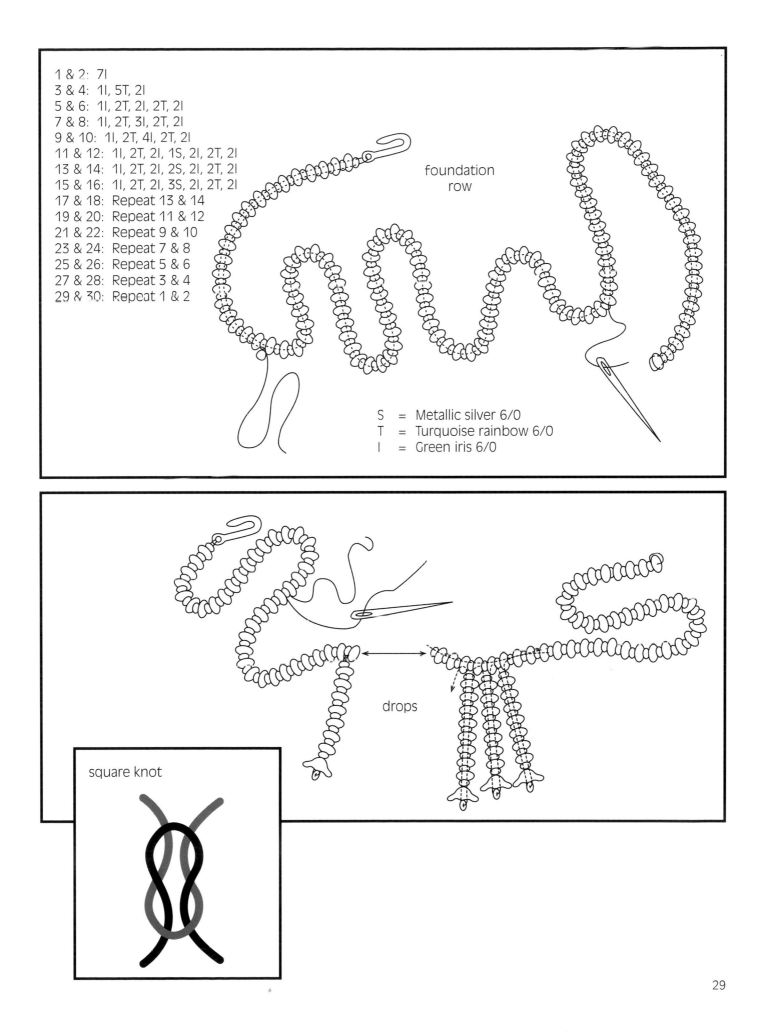

1 & 2: 7I
3 & 4: 1I, 5T, 2I
5 & 6: 1I, 2T, 2I, 2T, 2I
7 & 8: 1I, 2T, 3I, 2T, 2I
9 & 10: 1I, 2T, 4I, 2T, 2I
11 & 12: 1I, 2T, 2I, 1S, 2I, 2T, 2I
13 & 14: 1I, 2T, 2I, 2S, 2I, 2T, 2I
15 & 16: 1I, 2T, 2I, 3S, 2I, 2T, 2I
17 & 18: Repeat 13 & 14
19 & 20: Repeat 11 & 12
21 & 22: Repeat 9 & 10
23 & 24: Repeat 7 & 8
25 & 26: Repeat 5 & 6
27 & 28: Repeat 3 & 4
29 & 30: Repeat 1 & 2

foundation
row

S = Metallic silver 6/0
T = Turquoise rainbow 6/0
I = Green iris 6/0

drops

square knot

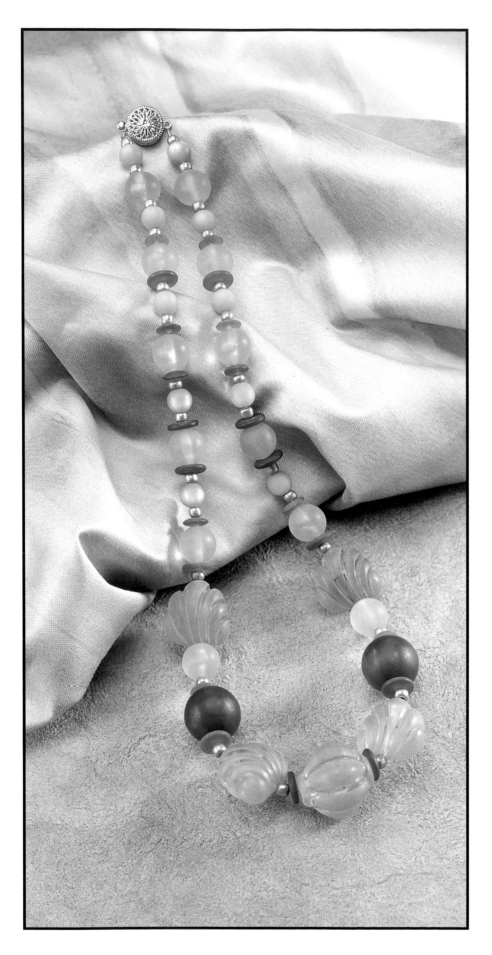

lavender matte necklace

Materials:

An assortment of similar beads,
  roughly graduated in size;
  enough to make an
  18" necklace
Spacer beads
Twenty-four inches of 25 lb.
  test nylon fishing line
Two gold-tone crimps
One gold-tone clasp
  with eyelets

Beading:

This type of necklace sometimes takes more time to plan
than to make. This is a good
example of using a "bead theme"
in a graduated necklace. The
theory behind the design is to
select an assortment of beads
with a common theme —
either texture, shape, material,
or finish. Then, they are com-
bined in a pleasing manner, with
the largest bead at the center
and the smaller beads graduating
out from the center in an identical pattern on both sides.

The pattern of "theme" beads
can be united using the same
small spacer throughout, in this
case, a small metallic gold 6/0
seed bead. Then, simply string
the beads onto the fishing line.

Following the directions for
crimping found in the General
Instructions on page 17, use
crimps to attach the fishing line
to the clasp.

If necessary, refer to the
photograph.

coil necklace

Materials:

One 35mm coil bead
Two 25mm coil beads
Two 20mm coil beads
Two 15mm coil beads
Two 10mm coil beads
Two gold-tone leather crimps
One gold-tone beehive clasp
Two gold-tone jump rings
Seventeen inches of
    4mm leather cord

Beading:

Thread the largest coil on the leather cord and center it. Add the next largest coils, one on each side of the largest, then add the two next largest on either side of that. Repeat until all the coils are grouped in the center of the leather cord.

Following the directions for crimping found in the General Instructions on page 17, attach the leather crimps to the ends of the leather cord.

Following the directions for attaching clasps found in the General Instructions on page 16, attach the clasp to the crimps using jump rings.

If necessary, refer to the photograph.

triple rainbow necklace

Materials:

About 275 flat wood disk beads,
    10 to 12mm diameter,
    in assorted colors
About 275 metallic gold
    6/0 seed beads
One gold-tone triple-hole clasp
Three 1-yard pieces of
    25 lb. test nylon fishing line
Six gold-tone crimps

Beading:

This is a "theme" necklace in which the design idea is carried through all three strands of the necklace. Simply string on an alternating pattern of wood disk beads and 6/0 seed beads, starting and ending with a 6/0 on each strand. Make three lengths: 17", 19", and 21".

Following the directions for crimping found in the General Instructions on page 17, use a crimp bead at each end.

Following the directions for attaching clasps found in the General Instructions on page 16, attach each strand to the clasp, taking care that they do not become twisted together.

If necessary, refer to the photograph.

beaded strawberry necklace

Materials:

One-inch cube of
  red polymer clay
1/2 oz. red luster
  11/0 seed beads
About 50 cream luster
  11/0 seed beads
About 120 dark green
  silver-lined 11/0 seed beads
One-inch scrap trimmed
  from a .028 headpin or
  eyepin or other wire
  suitable for a hanging loop
Eighteen inches of
  34-gauge brass wire
Clear nail polish
Hanging cord or ribbon

Beading:

Following the directions for
working with polymer clay found
in the General Instructions on
page 18, form the softened clay
into a strawberry about one-inch
tall. Lay the red seed beads out
on a flat surface in a tight layer
with all beads hole up. Roll the
strawberry shape in the beads,
and press the beads tightly into
the surface of the clay. Remove a
few red beads, and replace them
with cream beads to give the
appearance of strawberry seeds.
Repeat until the entire surface is
covered with beads, filling in with
individual beads as needed to
cover the entire surface.

Cut the brass wire into five
equal sections. Slip 20 dark green
seed beads on each wire. Twist
the wire ends together to form
five individual leaves. Twist all five
wires together just past the end
of the beads to form a bunch of
five leaves. Twist the "stem" until
the wire bunch becomes quite
stiff and trim to 5/8". Insert the

"stem" into the top of the
beaded strawberry until it
disappears. Press the sides of the
strawberry lightly to ensure the
firm attachment of the stem.

Form a U-shaped piece with
the headpin scrap and insert it
into the top of the strawberry

over the leaves — be sure to
leave enough space to slip the
hanging cord or ribbon through.

Bake according to General
Instructions, and allow to cool
before handling. Coat the entire
strawberry — leaves and hanger
excluded — with clear nail polish.

beaded pear necklace

Materials:

One-inch cube of
   light green polymer clay
1/2 oz. light green transparent
   rainbow 11/0 seed beads
About 50 dark green
   silver-lined 11/0 seed beads
One-inch scrap trimmed
   from a .028 headpin or
   eyepin or other wire
   suitable for a hanging loop
Six inches of
   34-gauge brass wire
Clear nail polish
Hanging cord or ribbon

Beading:

Following the directions for working with polymer clay found in the General Instructions on page 18, form the softened clay into a pear about one-inch tall. Lay the light green seed beads out on a flat surface in a tight layer with all beads hole up. Roll the pear shape in the beads, and press the beads tightly into the surface of the clay. Repeat until the entire surface is covered with beads, filling in with individual beads as needed to cover the entire surface.

Cut the brass wire into two equal sections. Twist the two wires together. Slip 10 dark green seed beads on each of the two outer wires and eight on each of the two inner wires. Twist the wire ends together just past the end of the beads to form a beaded leaf. Twist the "stem" until the wire bunch becomes quite stiff and trim to 5/8". Insert the "stem" into the top of the beaded pear until it disappears. Press the sides of the pear lightly to ensure the firm attachment of the stem.

Form a U-shaped piece with the headpin scrap, and insert it into the top of the pear over the leaves — be sure to leave enough space to slip the hanging cord or ribbon through.

Bake according to General Instructions, and allow to cool before handling. Coat the entire pear — leaves and hanger excluded — with clear nail polish.

blue on blue necklace

Materials:

Sixty-two 6mm clear blue
   round beads
Forty 10mm blue tubes
104 silver 6/0 seed beads
One silver-tone clasp
   with double eyelets
Four silver-tone crimps
25 lb. test nylon fishing line

Beading:

Assemble two 20" strands — one alternating round beads and silver 6/0 seed beads, the other alternating tubes and silver 6/0 seed beads.

Twist the strands together. Following the directions for crimping found in the General Instructions on page 17, attach the strands to the clasp using the crimps.

If necessary, refer to the photograph.

porcelain rose necklace

Materials:

One oval gold-tone medallion
Three white porcelain roses
Assorted pearls and crystals
Purple pre-strung beads
Twenty-five teardrop pearls
Seventy-four faux pearls (8mm)
420 faux pearls (3mm)
Lavender watercolor
Lavender acrylic paint
One gold-tone barrel clasp
25 lb. test nylon fishing line
Industrial strength glue

Beading:

Add color to the white porcelain roses using a lavender color watercolor. Glue as desired to the oval medallion. Glue different sizes of pearls and crystals to the medallion to make a pleasing arrangement.

Using purple pre-strung beads, secure the ends with glue. Each strand should measure 2 1/2". Leave 1 1/2" of string at the top. Tie a small teardrop pearl to the bottom of each strand. Place a dot of glue on the knots. Trim the strings when glue is thoroughly dry. Group together two sets of three strands. Twist strings together, and tie securely to the bottom of the medallion.

String the pearls onto the fishing line. Lay them out flat to make sure strands are even. Brush a lavender wash on the pearls using watered-down acrylic paint.

Following the directions for attaching clasps found in the General Instructions on page 16, attach the clasp at the top.

If necessary, refer to the photograph.

embellished lace necklace

Materials:

Lace appliqué
Pre-strung pearls
An assortment of teardrop pearls
An assortment of pearls
One silver-tone clasp
   with double eyelets
Four silver-tone jump rings
Nylon beading thread

Beading:

Using nylon beading thread, adorn the lace appliqué with the assortment of pearls. Attach the pre-strung pearls at the lower edge.

Sew two strands of pre-strung pearls to each side of the appliqué, making sure necklace will hang nicely.

Following the directions for attaching clasps found in the General Instructions on page 16, attach the clasp using the jump rings.

If necessary, refer to the photograph.

striped clay necklace & earrings

Materials:

Six colors of polymer clay
Black polymer clay
Two gold-tone cord end crimps
Four black 6/0 seed beads
Two gold-tone 1/2" eyepins
Two gold-tone 1 1/4" headpins
One pair of ear clips or posts
Eighteen inches of
   black leather cord
One gold-tone barrel clasp
Jewelry glue
Varnish, if desired

Beading:

Following the directions for working with polymer clay found in the General Instructions on page 18, make the clay beads and the dome-shaped earring pads. The clay beads for the necklace are the following sizes: the round bead should be 1" in diameter and the two rectangular beads should be 3/4" x 5/8" x 5/8". The clay beads for the earrings should be 5/8" x 3/8" x 3/8".

Insert the eyepins into the earring pads, and make holes in the beads. The holes in the necklace beads should be large enough to accommodate the leather cord, while the holes in the earring beads need only accommodate the headpins.

Slip the three necklace beads onto the leather cord, and trim it to a 16" length. Following the directions for crimping found in the General Instructions on page 17, attach the crimp ends to the leather cord.

Following the directions for attaching clasps found in the

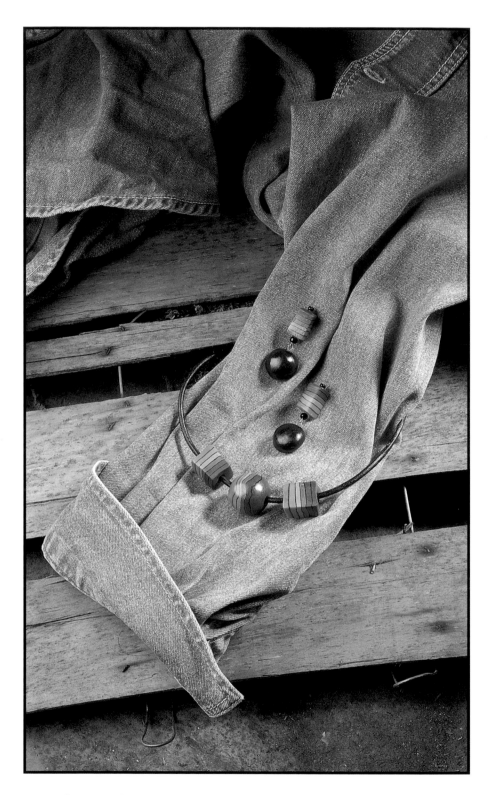

General Instructions on page 16, attach the clasp.

Following the directions for assembling beaded connectors found in the General Instructions on page 16, assemble the earrings. Slip one 6/0 seed bead, the large earring bead, and another 6/0 seed bead onto each headpin

and trim to 3/8" excess. Form a loop in the excess and close it around the eyepin on the earring pads.

Glue the ear clips or posts onto the back of the earring pads. Glaze all beads with varnish, if desired.

green yipes stripes necklace, bracelet & earrings

Materials:

One 15mm purple round
    plastic bead
Thirty 8mm frosted
    amethyst rondelles
114 frosted green
    6/0 seed beads
105 purple 11/0 seed beads
Twelve 10mm striped cubes or
    handmade beads using
    polymer clays
Two 18mm frosted purple
    end-drilled disks
Two gold-tone spring clasps
Two gold-tone split rings
Four gold-tone crimps
Two gold-tone headpins
One pair of ear clips or posts
25 lb. test nylon fishing line

Beading:

String the beads for the
necklace and the bracelet.
    Following the directions for
crimping found in the General
Instructions on page 17, attach
the crimps to the fishing line.
    Following the directions for
attaching clasps found in the
General Instructions on page 16,
attach the clasp.
    Following the directions for
assembling beaded connectors
found in the General Instructions
on page 16, assemble the
earrings. Slip the beads onto
each headpin, and trim to 3/8"
excess. Form a loop in the
excess, and close it around
the disks.
    Glue the ear clips or posts
onto the back of the disks.

lilac tassel necklace & earrings

Materials:

Three 15mm sub-opaque white
    side-drilled plastic disks
582 lilac 11/0 seed beads
456 white 11/0 seed beads
Twenty-four bronze
    11/0 seed beads
Three gold-tone end caps
Two gold-tone headpins
Four gold-tone eyepins
Two gold-tone crimps
One gold-tone spring clasp
One gold-tone split ring
One pair of ear clips or posts
Sewing thread
25 lb. test nylon fishing line
Jewelry glue

Beading:

Make the three tassels. Each
tassel has eight rows of beads
strung onto thread. Use one
bronze seed bead to anchor the
bottom of each row of beads.
Following the bronze seed bead,
add three lilac seed beads, one
white seed bead, two lilac seed
beads, one white seed bead, one
lilac seed bead, two white seed
beads, one lilac seed bead, 12
white seed beads.

Following the directions for
attaching end caps found in the
General Instructions on page 16,
attach the tassels to the end caps.
Attach the end caps to the
side-drilled plastic disks.

String the lilac seed beads onto
the fishing line, making a 19"
strand. Following the directions for
crimping found in the General
Instructions on page 17, attach
the clasp using the crimps.

Attach one disk and tassel onto
the center of the strand. Glue the
ear clips or posts onto the back of
the side-drilled plastic disks.

If necessary, refer to the
photograph.

indian agate necklace & earrings

Materials:

Three 9x15mm matte gold beads
Two 7x13mm matte gold beads
Twelve 6mm matte gold beads
Fourteen 5x8mm
   matte gold beads
Ten 6x15mm matte gold beads
Ten 10mm indian agate beads
Twelve 6mm indian agate beads
Eighteen 4mm
   indian agate cubes
One gold-tone hook clasp
One gold-tone split ring
Two gold-tone headpins
One pair of matte gold-tone
   5/8" hoop earring posts

Beading:

The design shown uses round and twisted corrugated beads — lined surface similar to corduroy or box cardboard.

This necklace is made of graduated alternating matte gold and indian agate beads. Any pattern of stringing can be used, but start at the center of the necklace with the larger beads and gradually decrease the size as stringing out toward the clasp in an identical pattern on both sides. This will create a pleasing look which hangs nicely.

String the beads to a length of 22".

Following the directions for crimping found in the General Instructions on page 17, attach the clasp using the crimps.

Following the directions for assembling beaded connectors found in the General Instructions on page 16, assemble the earrings.

If necessary, refer to the photograph.

yin-yang necklace, bracelet & earrings

Materials:

Nine 3/4" metal yin-yang beads
Eleven 8mm black onyx beads
Two 1" silver tube beads
244 black 11/0 seed beads
Four 4mm silver-tone beads
Four blue 11/0 seed beads
Two silver-tone beehive clasps
Four silver-tone crimps
Two silver-tone headpins
One pair of silver-tone ear wires
25 lb. test nylon fishing line

Beading:

Cut a length of fishing line about 20" long. Place the center beads on the necklace. On each side of the center beads, add 7 inches of black seed beads.

Cut a length of fishing line about 10" long to make the bracelet. Start with one 8mm onyx bead, then add one yin-yang bead. Repeat the onyx/yin-yang pattern until there are six yin-yang beads. End with an onyx bead.

Following the directions for crimping found in the General Instructions on page 17, attach both ends of the clasp to the necklace and the bracelet using the crimps.

Following the directions for assembling beaded connectors found in the General Instructions on page 16, thread the beads onto the headpins in the following order: one blue 11/0 seed bead, one 4mm bead, one yin-yang bead, one 4mm bead, one blue 11/0 seed bead. Trim the excess to 3/8" and form a loop on each headpin. Close the loops around the loops on the wires.

jingle bells necklace & earrings

Materials:

Twenty to thirty small metal
open-end bells in
assorted colors and sizes
Thirty to forty metal
jingle bells in
assorted colors and sizes
Approximately twenty 6mm
cobalt blue faceted crystals
Two gold 6/0 seed beads
One 18" gold-tone chain
with large links
(4 to 5 links per inch)
Twenty-four inches of
green niobium wire
One gold-tone clasp
One pair gold-tone ear wires

Beading:

Lay out the design before
beginning to attach the bells to
the chain. Cut the niobium wire
in 3/4" lengths to make the
figure-eight connectors and
in 1 1/8" lengths for the
beaded connectors.

Arrange the bells so that the
pattern is roughly graduated.
Following the directions for
assembling beaded connectors
found in the General Instructions
on page 16, attach each large bell
with a cobalt blue crystal
beaded connector.

Between the larger bells,
attach smaller bells with simple
figure-eight connectors.

When attaching the bells, be
sure the chain links are flat and
untwisted so that they will
hang nicely.

Assemble two beaded
connectors that have one gold
seed bead each. Attach each one
to a jingle bell, and hang from
the inside of an open-end bell.
Attach to the ear wires.

pearl spray earrings

Materials:

One pair of silver-tone
   French ear wires
Two long silver-tone cone ends
Twelve silver-tone 2" headpins,
   .021 gauge
Two silver-tone 4" headpins
Fourteen 5mm fine-quality
   freshwater pearls

Beading:

Thread the pearls onto the headpins. Make two bunches — each will have six 2" headpins and one 4" headpin. Vary the ends randomly, and twist all seven headpins together. When the bunch is stable, trim all but the longest headpin so they will fit inside the cone end. Insert the longest end through the hole in the cone end, and trim so there is an excess of 3/8". Form a loop in the end of the headpin using round-nose pliers, and close the loop around the French ear wire.

If necessary, refer to the diagram below and the photograph.

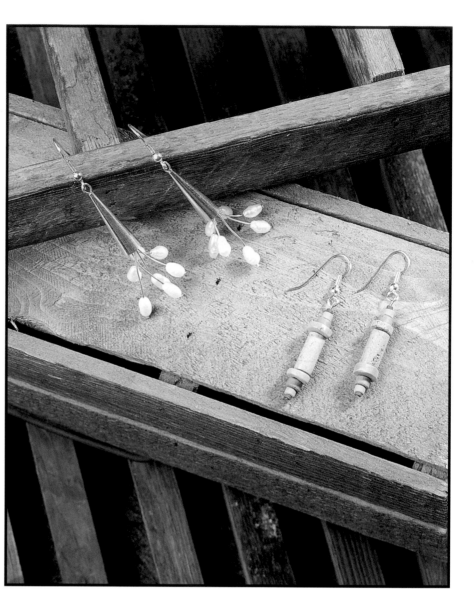

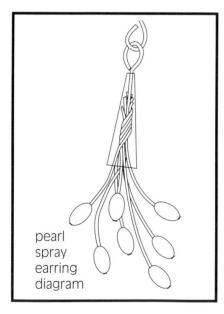

pearl
spray
earring
diagram

turquoise drop earrings

Materials:

One pair of silver-tone
   French ear wires
Two silver-tone 2" headpins
Two 7x15mm turquoise tubes
Four flat turquoise disks,
   10mm diameter x 3mm deep
Four dusty green ceramic beads,
   5mm diameter x 3mm deep
Four dusty blue ceramic beads,
   3mm cylinders
Four 2mm dark blue
   ceramic disks

Beading:

Following the directions for assembling beaded connectors found in the General Instructions on page 16, thread the beads onto the headpins in the following order: one 2mm ceramic disk, one 3mm ceramic bead, one 5mm ceramic bead, one 10mm turquoise disk, one turquoise tube, one 10mm turquoise disk, one 5mm ceramic bead, one 3mm ceramic bead, one 2mm ceramic disk. Trim the excess to 3/8". Form a loop in the end of each headpin using round-nose pliers, and close the loops around the French ear wires.

If necessary, refer to the photograph.

amethyst cabochon earrings

Materials:

One pair of ear clips or posts
Two 18x13mm
     amethyst cabochons
Two 18x13mm gold-tone
     lace-edged bezel cups
Two freshwater pearls
Two 10mm square
     turquoise matte glass beads
Two 12mm amethyst
     matte glass beads
Four 8mm amethyst
     matte glass beads
Six amethyst matte rainbow
     6/0 seed beads
Eighteen metallic gold
     11/0 seed beads
Twenty-eight matte turquoise
     rainbow 11/0 seed beads
Six gold-tone headpins
Jewelry glue

Beading:

Bend out three loops at the bottom of both bezel cups. Glue the amethyst cabochons in the bezel cups.

Following the directions for assembling beaded connectors found in the General Instructions on page 16, assemble the beaded connectors. Thread the beads onto the headpins. Refer to the photograph. Trim the excess to 3/8". Form a loop in the end of each headpin using round-nose pliers, and close the loop around the loops in the bottom of the bezel cups.

zuni bear earrings

Materials:

One pair of gold-tone
     French ear wires
Two 3/4" three-hole
     disk components
Six gold-tone 1" headpins
Two side-drilled turquoise chips
Ten turquoise chips
Two 8mm frosted
     amethyst rondelles
Four blue 6/0 seed beads
Two matte pink ceramic donuts
Four 12mm rose ceramic tubes

Beading:

Following the directions for assembling beaded connectors found in the General Instructions on page 16, assemble the beaded connectors. Refer to the photograph. Trim the excess to 3/8". Form a loop in the end of each headpin using round-nose pliers, and close the loops around the disk components.

Attach the ear wires to the disk components.

silver heart earrings

Materials:

One pair of five-hole
   silver-tone heart
   post earrings
Ten silver-tone 2 1/2" headpins
Twenty-two small dome-shaped,
   side-drilled freshwater pearls
Ten 4x10mm amethyst
   AB glass tubes
Two purple or amethyst
   fancy glass beads,
   about 12mm
Approximately 112 purple iris
   hex beads

Beading:

Following directions for
assembling beaded connectors
found in the General Instructions
on page 16, thread the beads
onto the headpins in the following order from the bottom: one
pearl, one tube, one pearl, hex
beads to fill the headpin. The
center beaded connector should
be beaded in the following order
from the bottom: one pearl, one
fancy glass bead, one pearl, one
tube, one pearl, hex beads to fill
the headpin. Trim the excess to
3/8". Form a loop in the end of
each headpin using round-nose
pliers, and connect the loops to
the ear posts.

If necessary, refer to the
photograph.

turquoise cabochon earrings

Materials:

One pair of matte silver-tone
   3/4" ear hoop earring posts
Two silver-tone
   figure-eight connectors
Two 18x13mm
   turquoise cabochons
Two 18x13mm silver-tone
   lace-edged bezel cups
Jewelry glue

Beading:

Bend out one loop at either
end of both bezel cups. Glue
the turquoise cabochons in
the bezel cups, and secure the
loops around the bezel cups. Use
the figure-eights, and attach one
end of each connector to the
loops on the bezel cups. Attach
the other end of each connector
to the ear posts. Twist one loop
on each figure-eight connector
so the cabochons hangs facing
front, perpendicular to the
ear posts.

If necessary, refer to the
photograph.

sun-star earrings

Materials:

One pair of gold-tone star
ear posts with loops
Two gold-tone sun face
drops with loops
Two gold-tone 1" eyepins
Two freshwater pearls

Beading:

If star ear posts cannot be
found, make them from
polymer clay.

Following the directions for
assembling beaded connectors
found in the General Instructions
on page 16, assemble the
beaded connectors using the
freshwater pearls and the
eyepins. Use the beaded connectors to attach the sun face drops
to the star ear posts. Carefully
close the loops.

sand dollar earrings

Materials:

One pair of silver-tone
sand dollar ear posts
Two large floral lamp beads
Two white 6/0 seed beads
Two silver-tone 1" headpins

Beading:

Following the directions for
assembling beaded connectors
and for embellishing simple
objects found in the General
Instructions on pages 16 and 17,
assemble the beaded connectors
using the lamps beads, seed
beads, and the eyepins.

Attach the beaded connectors
to the sand dollar ear posts.
Carefully close the loops.

If necessary, refer to the
photograph.

french wire earrings

Beading:

These earrings are made using finely coiled wire, known as French wire. It is extremely flexible and can be slipped over a shaped headpin quite easily. All three designs are created by following these simple steps:

1. Slip on the bottom bead(s).
2. Shape the headpin into the desired shape.
3. Slip on the French wire, and cut it using wirecutters. Be careful not to cut through the headpin. Only the slightest pressure is needed to make enough of a nick to separate the wire.
4. Trim the headpin to 3/8" beyond the end of the French wire.
5. Form a loop in the end of the headpin using round-nose pliers, and close the loop around the ear finding.
6. Shape the wires as desired.

If necessary, refer to the photograph.

... with freshwater pearls

Materials:

One pair of 4mm
    gold-tone ball and
    loop ear posts
Gold-tone French wire
Two large freshwater pearls
Two 4mm gold-tone beads
Two gold-tone 2 1/2" headpins

... with purple crystals

Materials:

One pair of purple niobium
    French ear wires
Gold-tone French wire
Two 5x7mm purple iris
    teardrop crystals
Two gold-tone 2" headpins

... with goldstone beads

Materials:

One pair of 4mm
    silver-tone ball and
    loop ear posts
Silver-tone French wire
Two 4mm goldstone beads
Two metallic silver
    11/0 seed beads
Two silver-tone 2 1/2" headpins

polymer clay earrings

Beading:

Follow the directions for working with polymer clay found in the General Instructions on page 18.

Using a pasta machine or rolling pin, roll the clay flat to a depth of 1/16". Using the cabochon as a guide, cut a circle out of the rolled clay. Place this cut layer over another layer of clay, and trim the edges into the appropriate shapes. Gently shape the petals with your fingers to round them.

Insert the cabochon into the cut hole again. Form additional petals or tiny balls of clay, and place them around the edge of the cabochon hole.

Insert the eyepin into the clay between two petals prior to baking. Form additional beads if necessary. Insert the headpins through the clay beads.

Following the directions for assembling beaded connectors found in the General Instructions on page 16, thread the beads onto the headpins. Trim the excess to 3/8". Form a loop in the end of each headpin using round-nose pliers, and connect the loops to the eyepins.

Bake according to the General Instructions, and varnish before assembling.

If necessary, refer to the photograph.

... sunflowers

Materials:

One pair of ear clips or posts
Yellow polymer clay
Two 12mm black onyx
    round cabochons
Four black 6/0 seed beads
Two gold-tone 1/2" eyepins
Two gold-tone 1 1/2" headpins
Jewelry glue
Gloss varnish

... anemones

Materials:

One pair of ear clips or posts
Dark blue polymer clay
Two 12mm rose quartz
    round cabochons
Two 4x15mm rose quartz tubes
Two gold-tone 1/2" eyepins
Two gold-tone 1 1/4" headpins
Jewelry glue
Gloss varnish

... marigold

Materials:

One pair of ear clips or posts
Rose polymer clay
Two 18x13mm amethyst cabochons
Two 12mm amethyst glass crystals
Four small dome-shaped
    freshwater pearls
Two gold-tone 1/2" eyepins
Two gold-tone 1" headpins
Jewelry glue
Gloss varnish

... blue/white

Materials:

One pair of ear clips or posts
White polymer clay
Two 18x13mm blue-lace
    agate cabochons
Two 10 to 12mm blue-lace
    agate beads
Two gold-tone 1/2" eyepins
Two gold-tone 1" headpins
Jewelry glue
Gloss varnish

hex earrings

Beading:

Following the directions for brick-stitching found in the General Instructions on page 17, weave the main body of the earrings.

Add the hangers when the body is complete. Attach the completed earring to the ear post using double-sided adhesive dots or glue.

If necessary, refer to the photograph.

... pastel crystal hex

Materials:

One pair of ear clips or posts
Eighty medium pink luster
    11/0 seed beads
Eighty lavender luster
    11/0 seed beads
Fifty-six light lavender luster
    11/0 seed beads
Twenty-six metallic gold
    11/0 seed beads
Eight 4mm clear lavender
    English cuts
Two 8mm clear lavender
    English cuts
Double-faced adhesive dots
    or jewelry glue

... english cut hex

Materials:

One pair of ear clips or posts
Seventy medium blue luster
    11/0 seed beads
Forty-six aqua luster
    11/0 seed beads
Sixty light green luster
    11/0 seed beads
Forty-two metallic gold
    11/0 seed beads
Ten 4mm aqua English cuts
Double-faced adhesive dots
    or jewelry glue

... black & turquoise hex

Materials:

One pair of ear clips or posts
Eighty-two matte black
    11/0 seed beads
150 matte turquoise iris
    11/0 seed beads
Ten matte turquoise iris
    6/0 seed beads
Double-faced adhesive dots
    or jewelry glue

... blue & silver hex

Materials:

One pair of ear clips or posts
154 crystal silver-lined
    11/0 seed beads
Forty-four light blue color-lined
    11/0 seed beads
Thirty-four gold silver-lined
    11/0 seed beads
Ten light blue English cuts
Double-faced adhesive dots
    or jewelry glue

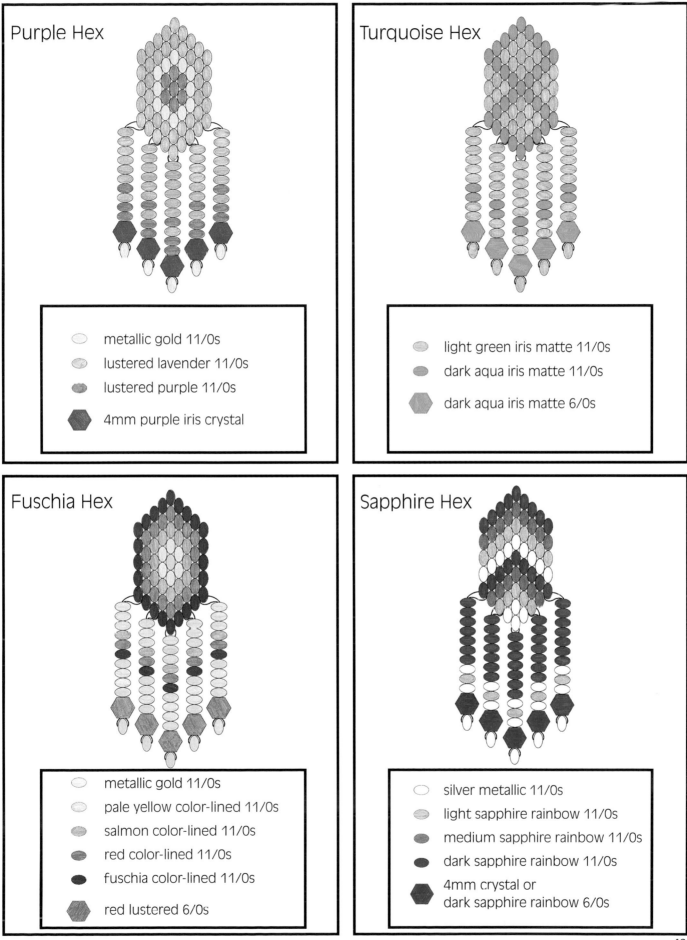

Purple Hex

- metallic gold 11/0s
- lustered lavender 11/0s
- lustered purple 11/0s
- 4mm purple iris crystal

Turquoise Hex

- light green iris matte 11/0s
- dark aqua iris matte 11/0s
- dark aqua iris matte 6/0s

Fuschia Hex

- metallic gold 11/0s
- pale yellow color-lined 11/0s
- salmon color-lined 11/0s
- red color-lined 11/0s
- fuschia color-lined 11/0s
- red lustered 6/0s

Sapphire Hex

- silver metallic 11/0s
- light sapphire rainbow 11/0s
- medium sapphire rainbow 11/0s
- dark sapphire rainbow 11/0s
- 4mm crystal or dark sapphire rainbow 6/0s

component earrings

Beading:

Simple components can be used to make elegant earrings. There is a nearly endless variety of types and styles of components. Each bead store and mail-order bead source will have a different variety, depending on the styles component manufacturers are making at the time. The techniques used in the styles shown will work with styles of the future.

Following the directions for assembling beaded connectors found in the General Instructions on page 16, assemble beaded connectors when necessary.

When using ear clips or posts, attach the completed earring to the ear post using double-sided adhesive dots or glue.

If necessary, refer to the photograph.

... decorative finding

Materials:

One pair of gold-tone
    stamped ear posts
    with three loops
Six gold-tone headpins
Twelve gold 11/0 seed beads
Six side-drilled amber chunks

... hollow cone

Materials:

One pair of silver-tone
    French ear wires
One pair of silver-tone cones
Two silver-tone headpins
Two spiral lamp beads

... hoop with interior drop

Materials:

One pair of silver-tone
    French ear wires
One pair of silver-tone hoops
Two silver-tone headpins
Two cinnabar beads

... cabochon mount

Materials:

One pair of silver
    stamped ear posts
    with bottom loops
    and 4mm cabochon opening
Two silver-tone headpins
Two 4mm amber
    round cabochons
Two freshwater pearls

... blue lace agate

Materials:

One pair of ear clips or posts
Two 15mm side-drilled
   blue lace agate disks
Two 10mm blue lace
   agate cubes
Four 4mm blue lace
   agate round beads
Four silver-tone headpins
Double-sided adhesive dots
   or jewelry glue

... indian agate

Materials:

One pair of ear clips or posts
Two 18mm side-drilled indian
   agate triangular flat beads
Two 4mm indian agate cubes
Two 10mm indian agate
   round beads
Four gold-tone headpins
Double-sided adhesive dots
   or jewelry glue

... cobalt drop

Materials:

One pair of ear clips or posts
Two 15mm sub-opaque white
   side-drilled plastic disks
Two 7x10mm cobalt
   drop crystals
Four white 11/0 seed beads
Four gold-tone headpins
Double-sided adhesive dots
   or jewelry glue

... blue lozenge

Materials:

One pair of ear clips or posts
Two 12x20mm blue lozenge-
   shaped plastic beads
Two 5x15mm twisted gold-tone
   finished bicones

Four cobalt 6/0 seed beads
Eight gold 11/0 seed beads
Four gold-tone headpins
Double-sided adhesive dots
   or jewelry glue

artistic dangle earrings

Beading:

Following the directions for assembling beaded connectors found in the General Instructions on page 16, and following the diagrams on page 53, assemble the components on headpins. Trim all headpins to 3/8" before forming loops and assembling.

If necessary, refer to the photograph

... stars & stripes

Materials:

One pair of silver-tone
   French ear wires
216 red 14/0 seed beads
408 white 14/0 seed beads
Ninety-eight navy blue
   14/0 seed beads
Two 3/8" white glass star beads
Thirty-four silver-tone
   3" headpins

... yin-yang

Materials:

One pair of gold-tone
   French ear wires
304 metallic gold
   14/0 seed beads
178 black 14/0 seed beads
Ninety white 14/0 seed beads
Two 12 to 16mm yin-yang beads
Thirty-four gold-tone
   3" headpins

... treble clef

Materials:

One pair of silver-tone
   French ear wires
476 white 14/0 seed beads
128 metallic silver
   14/0 seed beads
136 metallic bronze
   14/0 seed beads
Two music note or clef charms
Thirty-four silver-tone
   3" headpins

... heart

Materials:

One pair of gold-tone
   French ear wires
134 salmon 14/0 seed beads
220 green 14/0 seed beads
120 blue 14/0 seed beads
240 white 14/0 seed beads
Two heart charms
Thirty-four gold-tone
   3" headpins

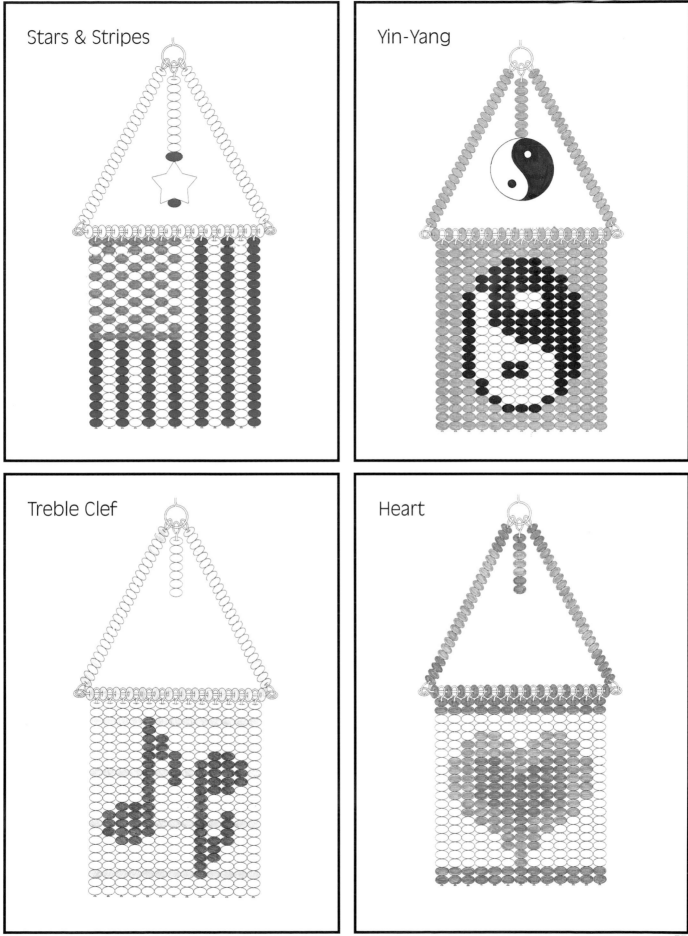

Stars & Stripes

Yin-Yang

Treble Clef

Heart

ear cuffs

Beading:

Following the directions for assembling beaded connectors found in the General Instructions on page 16, place the beads on the headpin and trim it to the desired length. Form a loop in the end of each headpin using round-nose pliers. Close the loops around the holes in the ear cuffs. Bend each headpin to make the drop hang nicely.

If necessary, refer to the photograph.

... with amethyst crystal

Materials:

One silver-tone ear cuff
One silver-tone 2" headpin
One 8mm amethyst crystal
Thirty-two metallic purple
   14/0 seed beads

... with teardrop crystal

Materials:

One gold-tone ear cuff
One gold-tone 1 3/4" headpin
Two metallic gold
   11/0 seed beads
One 4x7mm purple iris
   teardrop crystal

... with turquoise tube

Materials:

One silver-tone ear cuff
One silver-tone 2" headpin
Two metallic silver
   6/0 seed beads
One 4x10mm turquoise tube

... with freshwater pearl

Materials:

One gold-tone ear cuff
One gold-tone 1 3/4" headpin
1 1/4" gold French wire
One 5mm freshwater pearl

braided bracelet

Materials:

Seventy matte green iris
   6/0 seed beads
Seventy matte amethyst
   6/0 seed beads
Seventy matte purple iris
   6/0 seed beads
One gold-tone
   triple-loop bracelet clasp
Six gold-tone crimps
One yard of tigertail cord

Beading:

   Cut the tigertail cord into three equal lengths. Following the directions for crimping found in the General Instructions on page 17, attach each piece of the tigertail cord to one loop on the bracelet clasp. Thread all the beads of one color onto each strand of tigertail. After applying all the beads, tie a knot in the tigertail to keep them in place. This knot will be untied later.

   Braid the bead strands until their entire length is taken up. Refer to the diagram below. Keep the individual strands even with each other — do not let an imbalance occur. Untie the knot in the tigertail — one strand at a time — and attach each strand to the other side of the clasp using a crimp. Take care that the braid does not become twisted as this is done.

   If necessary, refer to the photograph.

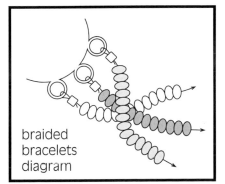

braided
bracelets
diagram

pastel braided bracelet

Materials:

Approximately 180 wood beads (5mm) in assorted pastel colors
One gold-tone triple-loop bracelet clasp
Six gold-tone crimps
25 lb. test nylon fishing line

Beading:

   Follow the directions for the braided bracelet above, using a random color pattern on each strand.

white disk bracelet

Materials:

Nine 15mm sub-opaque white
  side-drilled plastic disks
Assortment of colored
  6/0 seed beads
One gold-tone clasp
  with eyelets
Two gold-tone crimps
25 lb. test nylon fishing line

Beading:

Starting with a 6/0 seed bead, alternate disks and 6/0s on the fishing line, using the 6/0s in a random color pattern.

Following the directions for crimping found in the General Instructions on page 17, attach the clasp using the crimps.

If necessary, refer to the photograph.

button bracelet

Materials:

Eleven 1/2" antique buttons
One flat-link bracelet
Industrial strength glue

Beading:

Lay the bracelet out flat. If necessary, remove the shanks from the back of the buttons. Glue the buttons onto the bracelet. Be careful to evenly space the buttons.

If necessary, refer to the photograph.

peruvian bracelet

Materials:

Seven 15mm round
  peruvian style beads
Fourteen 6mm
  persimmon rondelles
Fourteen turquoise
  6/0 seed beads
Eight black 11/0 seed beads
One silver-tone beehive clasp
Two silver-tone crimps
25 lb. test nylon fishing line

Beading:

Thread seven repeats of beads onto the fishing line.

Following the directions for crimping found in the General Instructions on page 17, attach the clasp onto the ends using the crimps.

If necessary, refer to the photograph.

expansion bracelet

Materials:

One expansion bracelet blank
with 40 links,
each with three loops
About 120 headpins in a finish
matching the bracelet blank
120 assorted beads, pearls,
and crystals

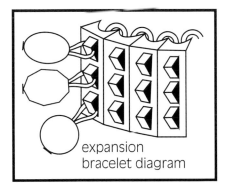

expansion
bracelet diagram

multi-bracelet bracelet

Materials:

One 2"-long bead in cup
with loops
One 1" bracelet clasp
One 3/4" bracelet clasp
Eighteen to 20 bracelets
and chains
Thirty-six 1/4" jump rings
Needle-nose pliers

Beading:

Using the needle-nose pliers,
shorten or lengthen the
bracelets and chains to the
same length.

Attach the bracelets to the
loops in the long bead using
the jump rings. Attach the
bracelet clasps.

If necessary, refer to the
photograph.

Beading:

The upper and lower rows are beaded with alternating pearls and
matte glass beads. The center row is beaded with a random assortment
of 6mm crystals.

Either complete each link of three beads, or work each row. It might
be easier to progress row by row or link by link. Trim each headpin so
there is slightly less than 1/2" of excess — more than the standard 3/8"
of excess will be needed. Form the excess into a loop, and close it
around the openings on each link.

If necessary, refer to the photograph.

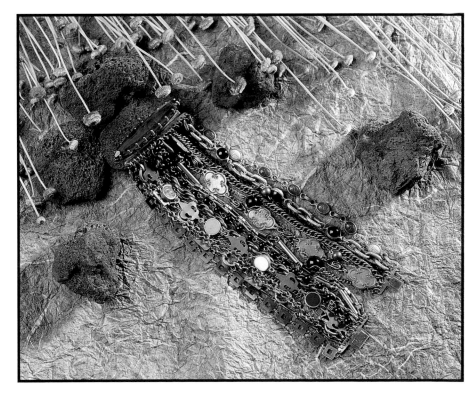

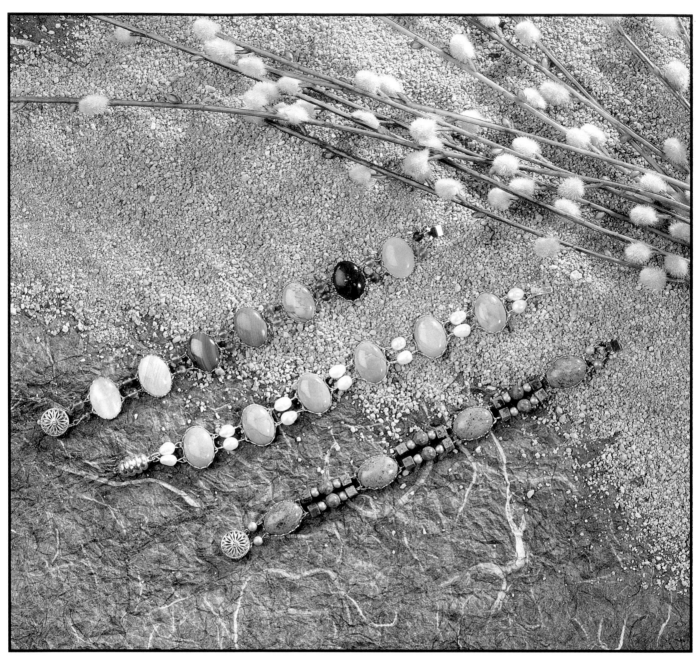

Pictured from top to bottom: Seven Cabochon Bracelet, Cabochon & Pearls Bracelet, Indian Agate Bracelet.

cabochon bracelets

Beading:

Bend four loops on each bezel cup, and mount and glue the stones as shown in the diagram.

Following the directions for assembling beaded connectors found in the General Instructions on page 16, assemble any beaded connectors that are needed and assemble the bracelet.

Following the directions for attaching clasps found in the General Instructions on page 16, attach the clasp to the bracelet.

If necessary, refer to the photograph.

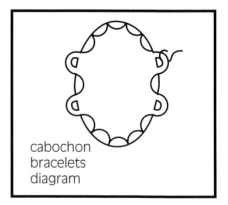

cabochon
bracelets
diagram

... seven cabochon

Materials:

Seven 18x13mm
    stone cabochons
    (model has rose quartz,
    blue lace agate, malachite,
    tigereye, turquoise, lapis lazuli,
    and serpentine)
Seven gold-tone
    lace-edged bezel cups
Sixteen 4mm fluorite
    round beads
Sixteen gold-tone 1" eyepins
One gold-tone clasp
    with double eyelets
Four gold-tone jump rings
Jewelry glue

... cabochon & pearls

Materials:

Six 18x13mm howlite
    dyed to look like
    turquoise cabochons
Six silver-tone
    lace-edged bezel cups
Fourteen freshwater pearls
Fourteen silver-tone 1" eyepins
One silver-tone beehive clasp
Jewelry glue

... indian agate

Materials:

Four 18x13mm
    indian agate cabochons
Four gold-tone
    lace-edged bezel cups
Twelve 4mm square
    indian agate beads
Six 6mm round
    indian agate beads
Sixteen 3mm gold-tone beads
Six gold-tone 1 1/2" eyepins
Four gold-tone 3/4" eyepins
One gold-tone clasp
    with double eyelets
Jewelry glue

silver & amethyst cabochon watch

Materials:

One silver watch face with
    five-loop side mountings
One silver bracelet clasp
Twelve 1" silver eyepins
Four 13x18mm silver
    lace-edged bezel cups
Four 13x18mm
    amethyst cabochons
Eight lavender
    6mm faceted crystals
Jewelry glue

Beading:

Make four figure-eight connectors, and attach one loop of each one to the second and fourth holes on the five-loop side-mounting.

On each bezel cup, bend out the loops as shown on page 58. Mount and glue the cabochons in the bezel cups.

On each of the remaining eight eyepins, slip on one lavender crystal. Trim the excess eyepin to 3/8", and form a loop to create a connector.

Assemble the watch band. Refer to the photograph.

liquid silver bracelet

Materials:

One 12mm ceramic tube bead
Two frosted amethyst
   6/0 seed beads
Two light green hex beads
Two aqua hex beads
Two lavender hex beads
Two pink hex beads
Two purple 11/0 seed beads
Sixty-four liquid silver beads
   (or more depending
   on desired length)
One silver-tone spring clasp
One silver-tone split ring
Two silver-tone crimps
Lightweight nylon fishing line

Beading:

Thread beads onto the fishing line in the following order: one purple 11/0 seed bead, one pink hex, one lavender hex, one aqua hex, one light green hex, one 6/0 seed bead, one ceramic tube, one 6/0 seed bead, one light green hex, one aqua hex, one lavender hex, one pink hex, one purple 11/0 seed bead. Add liquid silver beads to each side of the center motif to desired length.

Following the directions for crimping found in the General Instructions on page 17, attach the clasp at the ends using the crimps.

If necessary, refer to the photograph.

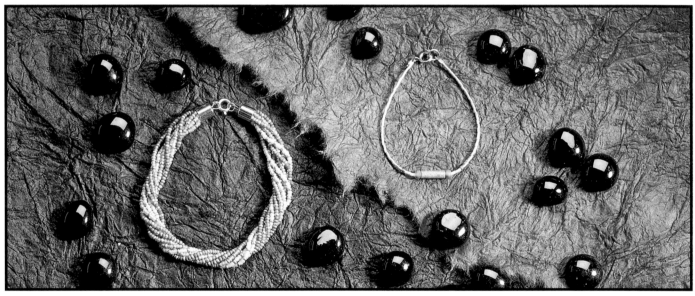

twisted bracelet

Materials:

392 gold 11/0 seed beads
Approximately 100
   11/0 seed beads in each
   of the following colors:
   turquoise, light aqua,
   champagne, teal iris,
   light green, dark purple,
   light gray iris, dark gray iris
Two gold-tone end caps
Two gold-tone
   figure-eight connectors
One gold-tone spring clasp
One gold-tone jump ring
Nylon beading thread

Beading:

String the beads on the nylon beading thread using the following pattern: one gold bead, two colored beads. Make eight 7 1/2"-long strands — one from each color.

Following the directions for attaching end caps and attaching clasps found in the General Instructions on page 16, attach the end caps and the clasp.

If necessary, refer to the photograph.

pearl anklet

Materials:

Thirty to thirty-five
   freshwater pearls
Forty silver-lined
   amber 14/0 seed beads
One gold-tone clasp
   with double eyelets
Two gold-tone crimps
Lightweight nylon fishing line

Beading:

Cut a 10" length of fishing line. Start with a silver-lined amber 14/0 seed bead, then alternate pearls and 14/0 seed beads until the desired length has been reached.

Following the directions for crimping found in the General Instructions on page 17, attach the clasp using the crimps.

If necessary, refer to the photograph.

coral anklet

Materials:

Forty to fifty-five coral chips
100 to 120 gold 11/0 seed beads
One gold-tone barrel clasp
Two gold-tone crimps
Lightweight nylon fishing line

Beading:

String the coral chips onto the fishing line alternately with two gold seed beads until the desired length has been reached.

Following the directions for crimping found in the General Instructions on page 17, attach the clasp using the crimps.

If necessary, refer to the photograph.

liquid silver anklet

Materials:

Enough liquid silver beads
   to make a 10" strand
One 8mm floral lamp bead
One silver-tone barrel clasp
Two silver-tone crimps
Lightweight nylon fishing line

Beading:

String 4 1/4" of liquid silver onto the fishing line. Add the glass bead, and continue with 4 1/4" more of liquid silver.

Following the directions for crimping found in the General Instructions on page 17, attach the clasp using the crimps.

If necessary, refer to the photograph.

floral oval pin

Materials:

Card stock paper
One freshwater pearl
Three light pink 6/0 seed beads
Four lavender 6/0 seed beads
Sixty-six gold #2 silver-lined
   bugle beads
11/0 seed beads:
   220 metallic gold
   150 black
   55 purple
   45 pink
   55 light blue
   35 aqua
   15 medium blue purple
   20 dark green
   20 medium green
One gold-tone pin back
Fusing web and backing fabric
Jewelry glue

Beading:

Transfer the design to the card. Following the directions for surface beading found in the General Instructions on page 19, stitch the metallic gold border outlines and the bugle beads first. Backtrack the outer gold row. Stitch the pearls and 6/0 seed beads in the center motif, then add the additional seed beads. Fill in the background with black seed beads.

Following the directions for fusing fabric found in the General Instructions on page 17, fuse the fabric backing to the back of the pin. Carefully trim away the excess card.

Glue the pin back to the center back of the pin.

If necessary, refer to the photograph.

Pictured from top to bottom: Floral Oval Pin, Oval Flower Pin, Petite Paisley Pin.

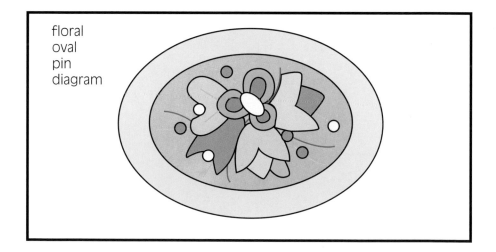

floral oval pin diagram

petite paisley pin

Materials:

Card stock paper
Four freshwater pearls
Eight matte topaz rainbow
  iris #2 bugle beads
11/0 seed beads:
  Fifty-four matte purple iris
  Forty-four cream
  Fifty-five matte amber
  152 metallic gold
Sewing thread
One gold-tone pin back
2 1/2" square fusing web
2 1/2" square backing fabric
Jewelry glue

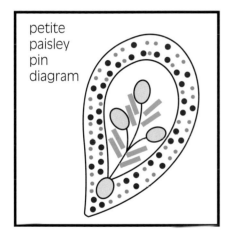

petite
paisley
pin
diagram

Beading:

Transfer the design to the card. Following the directions for surface beading found in the General Instructions on page 19, stitch the metallic gold outlines first, then add the pearls and bugle beads. Fill in the center background with the cream 11/0 seed beads, then stitch the three-bead clusters in the border.

Following the directions for fusing fabric found in the General Instructions on page 17, fuse the fabric backing to the back of the pin. Carefully trim away the excess card.

Glue the pin back to the center back of the pin.

If necessary, refer to the photograph.

oval flower pin

Materials:

Card stock paper
Six freshwater pearls
Two gold 6/0 seed beads
Fifty-four metallic gold
  11/0 seed beads
350 black 12/0
  three-cut seed beads
One 1 3/4" x 2"
  gold-tone oval frame
Sewing thread
One gold-tone pin back
Jewelry glue

Beading:

Transfer the design to the card. Trace the opening in the frame, and cut it out of the tracing paper. Center the frame around the traced floral spray design so that it is pleasing, and make an outline of the template to indicate the outer edge of the background beads.

Following the directions for surface beading found in the General Instructions on page 19, sew on the pearls, 6/0 seed beads, and metallic gold 11/0 beads. Fill in the background with black 12/0 beads using black sewing thread. The background of the piece may need to be colored in after the pearls have been stitched on to create a solid black appearance behind the black beads.

When the background is complete, carefully trim away the excess card. Avoid cutting any beading threads.

Glue the beaded piece into the frame. Glue the pin back to the center back of the pin.

If necessary, refer to the photograph.

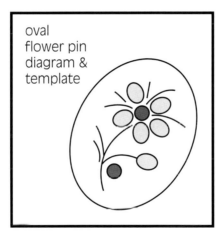

oval
flower pin
diagram &
template

cosmic
leather pin

Materials:

2" x 2" piece of pink leather
1 1/2" x 1 1/2" piece of
   turquoise leather
1" x 1" inch piece of blue leather
Five freshwater pearls
Eleven metallic gold 6/0 seed beads
Forty-three pink hex beads
One 6x12mm turquoise tube
Two side-drilled large
   turquoise chips
One gold-tone 2" eyepin
Five gold-tone 3" headpins
One gold-tone pin back
Jewelry glue

Beading:

Use the templates to cut the
leather pieces to the correct
size and shape. Glue the leather
pieces together to form one
three-layer unit.

Using a suitable sharp object,
such as a darning needle, pierce
the leather. The holes should be
large enough to accommodate
the diameter of the eyepin.
Insert the eyepin through the
holes until the loop is flush with
the first hole. Trim the other end
to 3/8", and form a loop with the
trimmed end. Bend the eyepin
slightly to allow the leather to lay
nearly flat. The assembled pin will
never lay entirely flat, and do not
attempt to make it do so.

Following the directions for
assembling beaded connectors
found in the General Instructions
on page 16, assemble the
headpin drops and trim the
lengths to 3/8" excess. Refer to
the photograph. Form loops with
the trimmed ends, and close the
loops around the eyepin and in
the end loops of the eyepins.

Glue the pin back to the top
center back of the pin.

If necessary, refer to the
photograph.

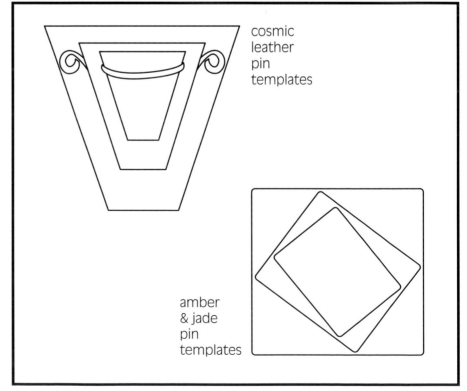

cosmic
leather
pin
templates

amber
& jade
pin
templates

amber & jade pin

Materials:

2" x 2" piece of bronze leather
2" x 2" piece of green leather
4" x 4" piece of rust suede
2" x 2" piece of fusing web
Four 10mm Chinese
   new jade beads
Four side-drilled amber chips
Eight gold 11/0 seed beads
Eight gold-tone headpins
Pin back
Jewelry glue

Beading:

Use the templates to cut the leather pieces to the correct size and shape. Cut two of the largest pieces, and fuse them together with fusing web to strengthen the base square. Glue the remaining leather pieces together to form one three-layer unit.

Following the directions for assembling beaded connectors found in the General Instructions on page 16, assemble the headpin drops. Glue the drops onto the assembled leather piece.

Glue the pin back to the top center back of the pin.

If necessary, refer to the photograph.

dangle charm pin

Materials:

Pin with loops
Chains
Seventeen to 20 charms or beads
Jump rings
Needle-nose pliers

Beading:

Using the needle-nose pliers, attach uneven lengths of chain to the pin loops using the jump rings. The chain lengths should range from 1 to 3 inches.

Using additional jump rings, attach the charms or beads to the bottom of the chains.

If necessary, refer to the photograph.

petit flower pins

... pansy

Beading:

Transfer the design to the card. Following the directions for surface beading found in the General Instructions on page 19, sew the seed beads onto the card. Backtrack the outer rows.

Following the directions for fusing fabric found in the General Instructions on page 17, fuse the fabric to the back of the stitched beadwork. Carefully trim around the edges with nail scissors.

Glue the pin back to the center back of the pin.

If necessary, refer to the photograph.

Materials:

Card stock paper
11/0 seed beads:
   12 yellow
   2 orange
   3 dark green
   57 medium purple
   200 light lavender
   57 dark purple iris
   23 medium orchid
One gold-tone pin back
Fusing web and backing fabric
Jewelry glue

... daisy

Materials:

Card stock paper
11/0 seed beads:
    18 bronze
    100 light orange
    112 medium yellow
    205 pale yellow
    27 light green
    30 medium green
One gold-tone pin back
Fusing web and backing fabric
Jewelry glue

... tulip

Materials:

Card stock paper
11/0 seed beads:
    27 dark purple
    58 medium purple
    56 light purple
    134 white
    17 dark green
    48 light green
One gold-tone pin back
Fusing web and backing fabric
Jewelry glue

... posy

Materials:

Card stock paper
One freshwater pearl
11/0 seed beads:
    60 red
    50 medium pink
    155 pale pink
    36 medium green
    28 light green
One gold-tone pin back
Fusing web and backing fabric
Jewelry glue

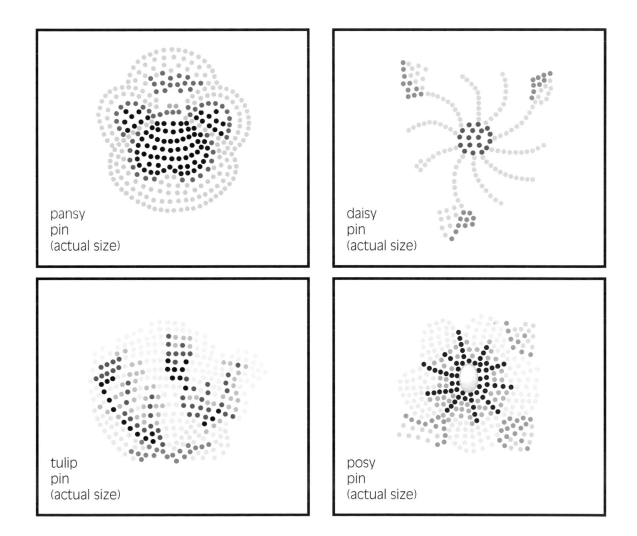

pansy
pin
(actual size)

daisy
pin
(actual size)

tulip
pin
(actual size)

posy
pin
(actual size)

Pictured from top to bottom: Cinnabar Stick Pin, Three-Drop Stick Pin.

three-drop stick pin

Materials:

One eyepin-topped
    silver-tone stick pin with
    end-stop
Three silver-tone 2 1/2" headpins,
    .021 gauge
One silver-tone eyepin
One 10mm silver-tone bead
One large freshwater pearl
One 6mm fancy glass bead
One 10 to 12mm
    fancy glass bead
Six-inch length of silver-tone
    French wire

Beading:

Following the directions for assembling beaded connectors found in the General Instructions on page 16, assemble the beaded connector using the 10mm bead and the eyepin. Slip the pearl onto one of the headpins. Trim off 1/2" of length. Cut a length of French wire 3/8" shorter than the length of the remaining headpin. Twist the headpin around the tip of a pencil to shape it into a loose spiral. Slip the length of French wire over the twisted headpin.

Form a loop with the 3/8" excess, and attach it to one end of the silver-tone-beaded connector. Repeat with the two glass beads, leaving one headpin untrimmed and trimming one 1/4". Attach the beaded connector to the loop of the stick pin.

If necessary, refer to the photograph.

cinnabar stick pin

Materials:

One blank threaded
    gold-tone stick pin with
    end-stops
One 14mm carved cinnabar bead
Smaller wood beads to
    reach the end of the pin
Jewelry glue

Beading:

Position the bead end-stop so that the selected beads will just cover the remainder of the stick. Place all but the last bead on the stick, then fill the hole of the last bead with glue. Place it on the end of the stick, then wipe away any glue which protrudes from the bead hole. Allow the glue to dry thoroughly.

If necessary, refer to the photograph.

rosary beads

Materials:

56" length of silver-tone chain with links large enough to accommodate the connector loops
Fifty-nine purple 8mm crystals
Eyepins to make 59 connectors
Twelve filigree bead caps
Four 3/8" metal coiled springs
One crucifix with loop
One Virgin Mary charm with three loops, one loop at 10 a.m., one loop at 2 p.m., and one loop at 6 p.m.
Three 4mm metal rings

Beading:

Assemble 53 beaded connectors, each one having one purple crystal. Assemble six additional beaded connectors with purple crystals bordered by filigreed bead caps.

Cut two sections of chain with 38 links each and assemble with crucifix drop. Join the two sections of chain with one ring; attach the ring to the bent-out end of one spring coil. Attach the crucifix to the other end of the bent-out coil. Refer to the photograph to attach two capped crystal connectors and three crystal connectors. Join the other end of the chains with one ring and attach it to the bent-out end of the spring coil. Attach the bent-out end of that spring coil to the 6 p.m. loop on the charm.

Join the other two spring coils to the additional loops on the charm. Attach the other bent-out end of the coil to two sections of the chain.

Lay the chain lengths out so they are parallel to one another. Attach five groups of ten crystals, separated by a capped crystal with a small space on either side. Trim the chain if necessary and join the other end of the two chains to a ring. Attach that ring to the spring coil.

chapter two

2

hair

bargello barrette

Materials:

Color-lined 11/0 seed beads:
- 128 yellow
- 84 aqua
- 45 orange
- 40 lavender
- 80 purple
- 8 salmon

One 3" barrette
Double-sided tape

Beading:

Following the directions for needle-weaving found in the General Instructions on page 18, weave the pattern as diagrammed.

Trim the double-sided tape to fit the barrette blank, and press it into place. Stretch the woven beadwork so that it fits the barrette, and press it into place. Press down firmly until the entire tape surface is in contact with the woven beadwork.

If necessary, refer to the photograph.

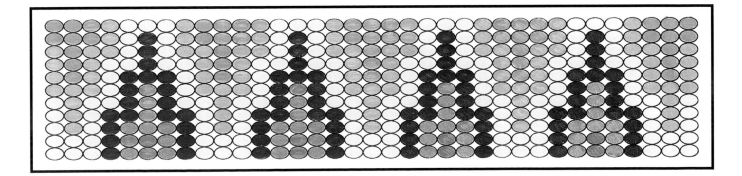

blue diamond barrette

Materials:

11/0 seed beads:
   113 dark sapphire rainbow
   176 light sapphire rainbow
   96 metallic silver
One 3" barrette
Double-sided tape

Beading:

    Following the directions for needle-weaving found in the General Instructions on page 18, weave the pattern as diagrammed.

    Trim the double-sided tape to fit the barrette blank, and press it into place. Stretch the woven beadwork so that it fits the barrette, and press it into place. Press down firmly until the entire tape surface is in contact with the woven beadwork.

    If necessary, refer to the photograph.

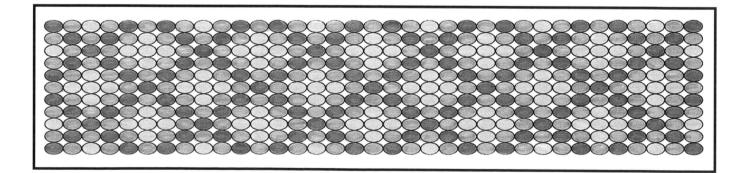

purple diamond barrette

Materials:

11/0 seed beads:
   91 amethyst color-lined
   16 salmon color-lined
   98 lavender
One 2" barrette
Double-sided tape

Beading:

Following the directions for brick-stitching found in the General Instructions on page 17, weave the pattern as diagrammed.

Trim the double-sided tape to fit the barrette blank, and press it into place. Stretch the woven beadwork so that it fits the barrette, and press it into place. Press down firmly until the entire tape surface is in contact with the woven beadwork.

If necessary, refer to the photograph.

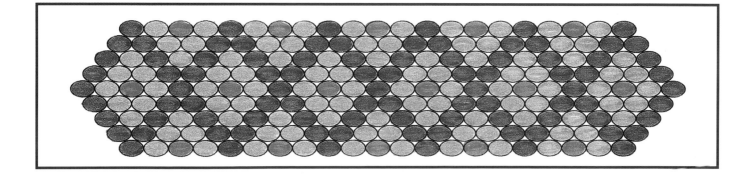

floral barrette

Materials:

11/0 seed beads:
   43 dark green
   60 light green
   36 purple
   12 gold
   90 light blue
   142 white
One 3" barrette
Double-sided tape

Beading:

Following the directions for needle-weaving found in the General Instructions on page 18, weave the pattern as diagrammed.

Trim the double-sided tape to fit the barrette blank, and press it into place. Stretch the woven beadwork so that it fits the barrette, and press it into place. Press down firmly until the entire tape surface is in contact with the woven beadwork.

If necessary, refer to the photograph.

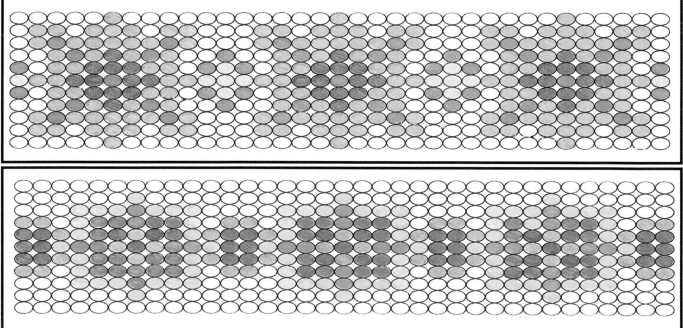

Try another floral design. Use bead colors of your choice.

tortoise shell barrette

Materials:

Thirty-six #2 iris bugle beads
Twenty-eight gold
  11/0 seed beads
Nine iris 6/0 seed beads
One 3 1/2" tortoise shell barrette
Jewelry glue

Beading:

Glue the beads onto the barrette. Starting in the middle, work your way out to each end. Refer to the photograph.

velvet rose ribbon barrette

Materials:

One velvet rose barrette
Fifteen to 20 assorted beads
Beading thread

Beading:

Thread the beads onto the beading thread, and randomly sew the lengths onto the back of the velvet rose(s) barrette.
  If necessary, refer to the photograph.

celtic
weave
comb

Materials:

11/0 seed beads:
    138 butterscotch color-lined
    71 off-white
One gold-tone 2" hair comb
Double-sided tape

Beading:

Following the directions
for brick-stitching found in
the General Instructions on
page 17, weave the pattern
as diagrammed.

Trim the double-sided tape to
fit the comb blank, and press it
into place. Stretch the woven
beadwork so that it fits the
comb, and press it into place.
Press down firmly until the
entire tape surface is in contact
with the woven beadwork.

If necessary, refer to the
photograph.

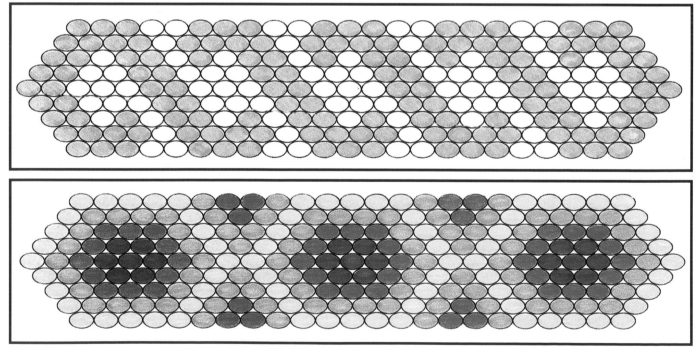

Try another celtic design. Use bead colors of your choice.

clinch combs

Beading:

Starting at the top of one side, thread the crimp onto the fishing line. Wrap around the side piece just above the first tooth of the comb.

Insert the end of the fishing line through the crimp and pull tight. Squeeze with pliers to flatten the crimp. Adjust the loop so that the crimp is at the back of the comb.

Thread on the beads, and wrap the fishing line around the back of the comb, catching the loose end in each wrap, then coming up between the next two teeth of the comb. Continue to add beads and wrap the fishing line around the comb so that one strand of the fishing line lands between each tooth, adjusting beads as necessary so they land on the top and outer sides of the comb.

Finish by threading on a crimp, winding the fishing line around one more time and putting the end through the crimp. Squeeze with pliers, trim off the excess fishing line, and repeat on the other side.

If necessary, refer to the photograph.

... multi-color

Materials:

Eighty-four pink 4mm English cuts
Eighty-four aqua 4mm English cuts
Eighty-four periwinkle blue
    4mm English cuts
Four crimps
Two yards of 25 lb.
    test nylon fishing line
One black clinch comb

... square beads

Materials:

Twenty-two aqua
    square wood beads
Twenty grape
    square wood beads
Four crimps
Two yards of 25 lb.
    test nylon fishing line
One purple clinch comb

... pink pearl

Materials:

Approximately 130
    4mm pink pearls
Four crimps
Two yards of 25 lb.
    test nylon fishing line
One white clinch comb

beaded hairsticks

Materials for each pair of hairsticks:

One pair of hairsticks
An assortment of beads
Acrylic paints
One gold-tone or
   silver-tone 2" headpin
Industrial strength glue

Beading:

Paint the hairsticks or leave natural, as desired. Thread the beads onto the headpins for the tip of the hairsticks. Trim excess headpin to 1" or to fit into the hairstick.

Place a small amount of glue between each of the beads to secure them to each other. Fill the hole in the hairstick with glue. Bend the headpin end slightly. Insert the headpin into the hairstick, and allow the glue to dry thoroughly.

If hairsticks are not available, chopsticks work great. A hole large enough to accommodate a headpin will need to be drilled into the top of each chopstick.

If necessary, refer to the photograph.

dangle hairsticks

Beading:

Thread the beads onto the eyepins for the tip of the hairsticks. Trim excess eyepin to 1". Fill the hole in the hairstick with glue. Bend the eyepin end slightly. Insert the eyepin into the hairstick, and allow the glue to dry thoroughly.

Following the directions for assembling beaded connectors found in the General Instructions on page 16, assemble the beaded connectors. Trim excess headpins to 3/8". Form a loop using round-nose pliers, and close the loop around the loop in the eyepin.

If necessary, refer to the photograph.

... emerald

Materials:

One 16x10mm
  blue and green glass tube
One 10x25mm
  blue and green oval glass bead
One 12x16mm amber bead
One 8x20mm foil lamp bead
Seven 4mm green crystals
Eighty-two silver-lined
  amber 14/0 seed beads
One gold-tone eyepin
Three gold-tone headpins
One hairstick
Jewelry glue

... turquoise

Materials:

One 12x18mm
  turquoise barrel bead
One 5x15mm turquoise tube
One 4x12mm turquoise tube
One 16mm turquoise rondelle
One 12mm fancy glass bead
Five 6mm matte amethyst
  glass rondelles
Two 10mm wood disks
Seven metallic gold
  6/0 seed beads
Sixty-eight metallic
  gold seed beads
One gold-tone eyepin
Three gold-tone headpins
One hairstick
Jewelry glue

... copal

Materials:

Four 10x8mm copal beads
Eight 5mm copal rondelles
Seven 4mm copal beads
Twenty-one 3mm wood beads
One gold-tone eyepin
Three gold-tone headpins
One hairstick
Jewelry glue

3

chapter three
wearables

pearl & lace collar

Materials:

One collar with lace trim
Fourteen white freshwater pearls
Three pink freshwater pearls
200 white 11/0 seed beads

Beading:

Transfer the placement lines to the collar with an embroidery pencil following manufacturer's instructions. Space as needed to fit.

Following the directions for surface beading found in the General Instructions on page 19, sew on the pearls and the seed beads.

If necessary, refer to the photograph.

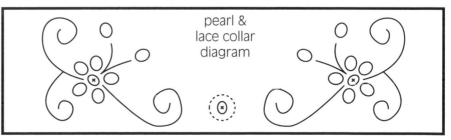

pearl & lace collar diagram

black lace collar

Materials:

One lace collar
4mm gold beads
Gold leaf-shaped beads
7mm black beads
Gold seed beads
Black seed beads
Black sewing thread

Beading:

Starting at the center front of the collar, hand-stitch each group of beads in place spacing them evenly around the collar. Work from the center of the collar to the sides. Make sure that each side of the design is even.

If necessary, refer to the photograph.

frosted amber pocket embellishment

Materials:

Shirt with pocket
Six freshwater pearls
One bronze 8mm crystal
Nineteen amber 6/0 seed beads
Four amethyst 6/0 seed beads
Eight amethyst 8/0 seed beads
One 20x25mm oval
    frosted amber cabochon
400 metallic gold
    11/0 seed beads
Leather
Fusing web

Beading:

Using the template, cut one octagonal piece each of the leather and the fusing web. Cut the center out of the leather as shown in the diagram, leaving the fusing web intact. Position the fusing web on the bead card, then position the leather over it with gold side up.

Following the directions for surface beading found in the General Instructions on page 19, bring knotted thread up from any number on the outer edge of the card, and thread on metallic gold beads until the beaded thread reaches the same number inside the circle. Repeat all around. Outline interior oval and outer octagon with metallic gold beads. As shown, sew the pearls and the large seed beads (anchored with small gold seed beads) directly over the leather using a small needle.

Attach hangers at the base of the embellishment. Position the oval cabochon in the center of the open oval space. Backtrack seed beads around the cabochon and outer edge. Fuse together according to manufacturer's directions. Melted fusing web will hold the cabochon in place. Be sure to hold hangers aside when trimming the excess from the bead card.

If necessary, refer to the photograph.

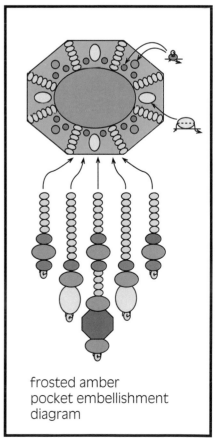

frosted amber
pocket embellishment
diagram

simple garment embellishments

jungle

Materials:

One animal pin with loops or
    openings for adding beads
Two extra small beads
Two small beads
Two medium beads
One large bead
Four flat beads
One 2 1/2" headpin
Needle-nose pliers

Beading:

Slide the beads onto the
headpin starting with the small-
est bead. Add the remaining
beads gradually getting to the
largest bead, then reverse the
order of the beads.

Using the needle-nose pliers,
make a loop in the end of the
headpin and attach it to the
opening in the animal pin.

cow skull

Materials:

One ceramic cow skull
Multi-colored seed beads
Small silver southwest charms
Silver jump rings
White acrylic paint
Brick red acrylic paint
Industrial strength glue

Beading:

String seven strands of multi-colored seed beads ranging from 4 to 7 inches in length. Add the charms to the middle of a few strands using the jump rings. Tie the strands off with a knot.

Fold each strand in half and tie a knot at the top of the doubled strands.

If a ceramic cow skull cannot be found, make one from polymer clay. Follow the directions for working with polymer clay found in the General Instructions on page 18.

Paint the skull with white acrylic paint and the horns with brick red acrylic paint. Let the paint dry thoroughly.

Glue the doubled strands of seed beads to the back center of the skull so that they hang at different lengths.

If necessary, refer to the photograph.

beaded collar & pockets

Materials:

Shirt or blouse with
  collar and pockets
Approximately 100
  4mm English cut or
  6/0 seed beads
  in a coordinating color
Approximately 100
  11/0 seed beads
  in a coordinating color
Sewing thread

Beading:

Using the technique shown below, sew the beads to the collar and the pockets of the shirt or blouse.

Space the beads 3/8" to 1/2" apart. Bury the finished thread inside the collar or pocket flap. Clip close, being careful not to cut the fabric.

If necessary, refer to the photograph.

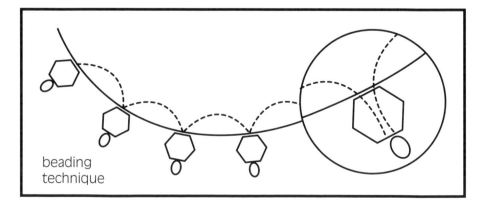

beading
technique

blazer cuffs & pocket

Materials:

Bugle beads in
   assorted sizes and colors
Seed beads in
   assorted sizes and colors
Sewing thread
Large beads, optional

Beading:

Starting at the top of the blazer pocket, randomly sew on the assorted bugle and seed beads close together. Allow the beads to become more sparse and uneven as you sew. This will give the beads the look of "falling snow."

If desired, replace the buttons on the blazer with large beads.

If necessary, refer to the photograph.

coin
dress

Materials:

One dress
Seventy-five to 80
   1" coin beads
Sewing thread
Straight pin

Beading:

Begin by marking the center of the neck on the dress with a straight pin.

Starting at the center of the neck and working out toward the shoulder seam, securely sew the coin beads on 3/4" apart in an even, consistent row around the neck opening. Repeat the process for the other side.

Repeat the process on the second row going only half way to the shoulder seams.

Repeat the process on the sleeve cuffs.

If necessary, refer to the photograph.

gloves

Materials:

One pair of gloves
An assortment of beads
Nylon beading thread or
    industrial strength glue

Beading:

Plan out the desired design with the assortment of beads. Following the directions for surface beading found in the General Instructions on page 19, sew the beads on the gloves. If preferred, the beads can be glued into position.

If you choose to use the designs shown in the models, refer to the photograph.

multi-color button covers

Materials:

Four 18mm button cover blanks
Four 12mm frosted
   round cabochons
Four different colors of
   11/0 seed beads
Four 12mm disks of
   double-sided adhesive
Sewing thread
Jewelry glue

Beading:

Begin by attaching the cabochon and needled double thread to the center of the button cover blank with the disk of double-sided adhesive. Slide enough beads onto the thread to snugly fit around the circumference of the cabochon. Slip the needle through the first three or four beads on the thread, and take up the slack.

Add a second row of beads around the first, and slip the needle through the first five or six beads on the second row. Run the needle back through the same beads in the opposite direction to secure the thread.

Carefully lift up the bead rounds, and apply glue to the surface of the button cover blank. Reposition the bead rounds so they are nestled into the glue. Allow the glue to dry thoroughly.

If necessary, refer to the photograph.

flat disk button covers

Materials:

Four 18mm button cover blanks
Four flat disk beads,
    larger than 18mm, but
    smaller than 25mm
Eight 1 1/2" headpins
Four 4x10mm tubular beads
Eight 4mm round beads
Eight 11/0 seed beads
    in a coordinating color
Jewelry glue

Beading:

Following the directions for assembling beaded connectors found in the General Instructions on page 16, slip each tubular bead onto a headpin and trim to 3/8". Form a loop with the excess.

Assemble the flat disk bead unit. Glue the assembly to the button cover. Allow the glue to dry thoroughly. Attach the beaded connector to the flat disk assembly and close the loops.

If necessary, refer to the photograph.

chapter four
decor
4

Glass heart box model pictured was made by simply gluing an assortment of rhinestones to the lid.

jeweled heart box

Materials:

One small heart-shaped box
covered with gold paper
or painted gold,
3/8" deep lid
Approximately 250 aqua
silver-lined #2 bugle beads
Approximately 600 gold
silver-lined 11/0 seed beads
Nineteen freshwater pearls,
3.5 to 4mm
One 25x40mm
Cape Amethyst cabochon
Three 4mm aqua faceted crystals
Industrial strength glue

Beading:

As shown in the diagram, glue the bugle beads and seed beads around the edge of the box lid.

Position the cabochon in the high center of the lid, and glue it in place. Glue a row of gold seed beads around the cabochon.

Position the three crystals as shown. Glue five pearls around each crystal in a flower shape. Between the flowers, glue bugle beads and pearls just outside the row of gold seed beads. Experiment with the positioning of the filler beads to make a nice fit. Allow the glue to dry thoroughly.

If necessary, refer to the photograph.

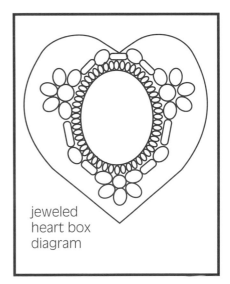

jeweled
heart box
diagram

pearl perfume bottle

Materials:

One glass bottle with
    2 1/2" x 3" work area
One 18x25mm faux
    mabe pearl cabochon
Nineteen cream 4mm faux pearls
Five blue 8mm faux pearls
Four butterscotch
    10mm faux pearls
Two butterscotch
    8mm faux pearls
Eighteen light green
    #2 bugle beads
Industrial strength glue

Beading:

Starting with the mabe pearl cabochon, glue the beads onto the bottle, then surround it with the 4mm faux pearls. Add all the bugle bead stems. When the stems and center mabe pearl groups are dry, add the remaining pearls to the stems.

Lay the bottle flat on its side while the glue dries to prevent slippage of the pearls. Allow the glue to dry thoroughly.

If necessary, refer to the photograph.

lace-covered round bottle

Materials:

One small round bottle
Lace
1/8" silk ribbon
One metal charm
An assortment of glass grape beads
Scissors

Beading:

Wrap the lace around the bottle, and tie around the neck of the bottle. Tie three or four lengths of silk ribbon around the top of the bottle. Bend the metal charm to fit over the ribbon and around the top of the bottle.

Using the scissors, gently curl the silk ribbon like curling ribbon. Trim the frayed ends.

Tie the glass grape beads to the ribbon, as desired.

If necessary, refer to the photograph.

94

silk ribbon charm bottle

Materials:

Thirty-six inches of thin gold wire
Approximately thirty-five assorted beads
Silk ribbons

Beading:

Secure a small bead to the end of the gold wire. Thread half of the beads onto the wire. Wrap it around the top of the bottle. Thread the remaining beads onto the wire and secure the last bead. Trim excess wire.

Wrap the wires and the beads around a pencil until you have curls.

Tie silk ribbons around the top of the bottle and trim the ends.

If necessary, refer to the photograph.

gold cord charm bottle

Materials:

One large three-sided bottle
Gold cord
An assortment of beads
An assortment of metal charms
Industrial strength glue or wire

Beading:

Wrap the gold cord around the lid, and tie it at the front.

Using glue or wire, attach an assortment of beads and metal charms below the knotted gold cord.

If necessary, refer to the photograph.

house magnet

Materials:

Sky blue polymer clay
#2 bugle beads:
   24 matte light topaz
   18 opaque white
   47 matte dark topaz
   19 satin green
   28 silver-lined light blue
Fifty-one matte green
   11/0 seed beads
Self-adhesive magnet strips
Varnish, if desired

Beading:

Following the directions for working with polymer clay found in the General Instructions on page 18, condition the clay and roll it out in a thin layer. Make a tracing of the design template, and use it to lightly outline the pattern onto the rolled clay.

Press the beads into the clay referring to the pattern shown. Do not press the beads too deep into the clay or they will disappear.

Bake according to the General Instructions, and coat with varnish, if desired.

Apply the magnet strips to the back of the piece.

If necessary, refer to the photograph.

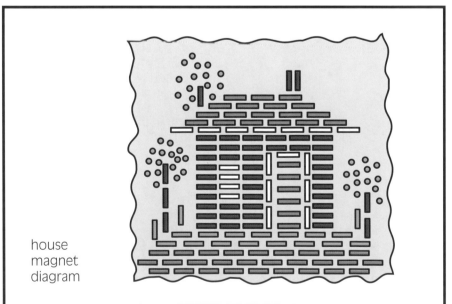

house
magnet
diagram

beehive stationery box & note cards

Materials:

Cardboard box with
   flip-up top
Note cards and envelopes
One permanent black
   fine-point marker
Assorted beads
Assorted charms
Industrial strength glue

Beading:

Draw a design on the top of the cardboard box and the note cards with a permanent black fine-point marker.

Glue the assorted beads and charms to the top of the card-board box and note cards, embellishing the designs.

If necessary, refer to the photograph.

butterfly stationery box

Materials:

Fabric covered
   cardboard box with lid
Two butterfly gift tags
An assortment of rhinestones
Industrial strength glue

Beading:

Glue the butterfly gift tags to the top of the cardboard box. Embellish the butterfly gift tags by randomly gluing on the rhinestones. Add additional rhinestones if desired.

jade tree
in clay pot

Materials:

14/0 seed beads:
   100 light orange
   Sixty lavender
Twenty light amethyst matte
   rainbow #2 bugle beads
One 2 oz. block of
   white polymer clay
One small clay pot,
   1 1/2" to 2" diameter
Roll of 34-gauge wire
Twenty aventurine chips
Ten amethyst chips
Five citrine chips
Five rose quartz chips
About forty undyed
   howlite chips
Four freshwater pearls
Double-sided adhesive tape
Jewelry glue

98

Beading the pot:

Cut six 3/8" diamonds of double-sided adhesive as shown in the diagram. Space them evenly around the top edge of the pot and press down. Do not remove the covering paper until you are ready to apply the beads. Following the pattern shown in the diagram, place 14/0 beads on the unpapered tape with the holes up. Press the beads into position when all are placed on the tape. Glue three vertical bugle beads together onto the pot between each diamond pattern. Allow the glue to dry thoroughly.

Assembling the bouquet:

Cut twenty-four 7" pieces of wire. Make two amethyst flowers, one citrine flower, and one rose quartz flower. For each flower, begin by centering one pale orange 14/0 bead on the wire folding the wire in half. Thread the doubled wire through a freshwater pearl and set it aside. Run one piece of wire through each of five chips (amethyst, citrine, or rose quartz), then double it. Twist all six doubled wires together to form one complete flower.

Using aventurine chips, make 19 strands as described for the flowers. Group them together in bunches of three, five, five, and six. Twist the groups together to form strands of leaves.

Gather all leaves and flowers together, positioning the leaves so the strands are shorter than the flowers. Twist all the leaves and flowers together to form a bouquet; pliers may need to be used to handle the entire bunch of wires. Check the height of the twisted bouquet against the height of the pot, and trim the wires so the bouquet is a nice height above the pot. Following the directions for working with polymer clay found in the General Instructions on page 18, soften the clay by working it in your hands, then wrap it around the wire bunch and press the assembly into the bottom of the pot. If there is too much clay, pinch some off so there is a 1/2" margin at the top of the pot. Level off the top of the clay. Bake the entire assembly at 200° F for 20 minutes to harden the clay. Allow the clay to cool completely. Pour a thin 1/8" layer of glue on top of the hardened clay, and cover the top of the clay with howlite chips to look like stone chips in a flower pot.

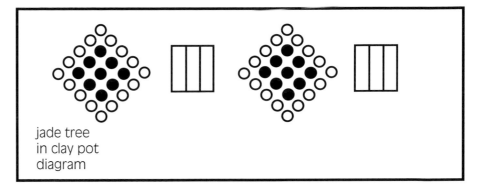

jade tree
in clay pot
diagram

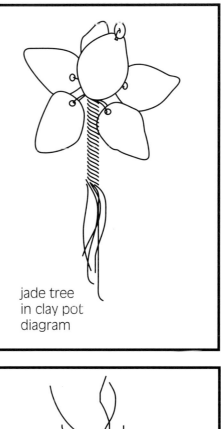

jade tree
in clay pot
diagram

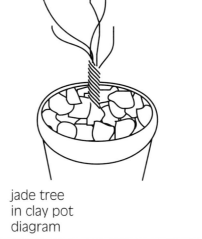

jade tree
in clay pot
diagram

aztec frame

Materials:

Small flat-surfaced frame
Four 18x13mm cabochons,
    acrylic or natural stone
Four 10mm flat disk beads
    of the same stone
    as the cabochons
One ounce of #2 bugle beads
About 75 metallic gold
    6/0 seed beads
About 100 metallic gold
    11/0 seed beads
About seventy-five
    11/0 seed beads
    of another color
Industrial strength glue

Beading:

Use any square or rectangular frame with a flat surface, and paint the surface, if desired. To adjust the design, simply lengthen or shorten the row of bugle beads which connect the cabochons and corner motifs.

Measure the sides to determine the center point of each side. Glue one cabochon centered on each side of the frame. Glue a row of 6/0 metallic gold beads around each cabochon. Allow the 6/0s to dry, then glue one 11/0 seed bead of another color in the center of each one, making sure the holes are sideways.

In each corner, glue one 10mm flat disk, and surround it with a single row of 11/0 metallic gold seed beads.

Connect the centered cabochons and the corner disks with a row of bugle beads. Allow the glue to dry thoroughly.

If necessary, refer to the photograph.

Use any color theme — the same design using rose
quartz cabochons and silver-lined lavender bugle beads
on a white frame will have a very feminine look.

The Angels
seem clothed with
golden plates,
constantly moving,
like
so
many
suns.

Pere Lamy

cherub frame

Materials:

Flat-surfaced 5x7 frame
Cherub gift tag
An assortment of
   small rhinestones
Decoupage
Brush
Gold acrylic paint, optional
Industrial strength glue

Beading:

Paint the frame with gold acrylic paint. Trim the gift tag to fit
the top of the frame. Decoupage the gift tag onto the frame following
manufacturer's instructions. Let the decoupage dry thoroughly.
   Randomly glue the rhinestones onto the gift tag and the frame.
If necessary, refer to the photograph.

vase

Materials:

One glass vase
An assortment of rhinestones
Toothpick
Industrial strength glue

Beading:

Lay the vase on a table and arrange the rhinestones into a desired design.

Starting at the top edge, glue on the rhinestones one at a time. Use the toothpick to apply the glue.

To achieve a straight line, an envelope or folded sheet of paper can be used. Make sure any excess glue is wiped off the vase.

If necessary, refer to the photograph.

cabochon & crystal votive cup

Materials:

One 2"-diameter votive candle cup
Eleven 10x15mm
    acrylic cabochons
275 crystal AB 11/0 seed beads
Industrial strength glue

Beading:

Glue the cabochons around the candle cup, adjusting them for even spacing before the glue dries — the cabochons will not lay perfectly flat. Allow the glue to dry thoroughly.

Run a thin bead of glue around each cabochon, and place the 11/0 seed beads with the holes perpendicular to the surface — complete each one before gluing the next. Adjust the beads before the glue dries. Allow the glue to dry thoroughly.

If necessary, refer to the photograph.

frosted votive cups

Materials:

Frosted votive candle cups
An assortment of beads
Wire or string

Beading:

String the beads onto the wire or string as desired, and tightly wrap the wire or string around the top of the votive cup under the rim. If desired, some of the wire or string with beads can be pulled down around the votive cup. Glue can be used to help tack the wire or string into place.

If necessary, refer to the photograph.

suncatchers

Materials for one suncatcher:

.021 gauge wire
An assortment of beads
Two fishing swivels
An assortment of crystals
An assortment of small charms
Industrial strength glue

Beading:

String the beads onto the wire, leaving 1 1/2" at the top to form a loop.

Add one fishing swivel, then an assortment of crystals. Hook the remaining fishing swivel to the top of the 15" length of wire, and string on additional beads under the swivel. Add small charms occasionally.

Bend the wire into a spiral shape as the beads are added. Tie the wire around the last bead, and secure it with glue.

If necessary, refer to the photograph.

Beading options:

Ornamental jewelry pieces often make the main focal point or base when making suncatchers.

Start with the base and create from there, stacking beads and attaching crystals as desired onto fishing line or thin wire. Use beads that are different shapes and sizes.

Antique crystals, chandelier crystals, and charms work great.

clear crystal napkin rings

Materials:

Metal napkin rings
An assortment of clear crystals
Gold-tone .021 gauge wire

Beading:

Randomly place the clear crystals on the wire, and wrap the wire around each metal napkin ring.

The rings do not have to be identical — the placement of the crystals adds a unique touch to each ring!

If necessary, refer to the photograph.

large round bead napkin rings

Materials:

Five large round beads of identical size in either the same color or, if desired, different colors for each ring
Gold-tone wire

Beading:

String the five large round beads onto the wire. Then, using the wire, randomly wrap the wire around the beads and in between the beads.

If necessary, refer to the photograph.

candles

Materials:

Two decorator candles,
   4" in diameter
An assortment of studs
   and rhinestones
Industrial strength glue

Beading:

Plan a design before beginning. Reference points can be marked on the candle by poking a pin into the wax.

Push the studs into the candle as desired. Glue on the rhinestones. Let the glue dry thoroughly.

If necessary, refer to the photograph.

crystal-drop
candelabra

Materials:

One candelabra
An assortment of tear-drop
  crystals in a variety of sizes
  (chandelier crystals
  work perfectly)
Several jump rings or wire

Beading:

  Using the jump rings or wire,
randomly attach the tear-drop
crystals to the candelabra.
  If necessary, refer to the
photograph.

sachet box, bag & pillow

Materials for box:

One 4 x 4 x 1 box without lid
One silk napkin or handkerchief
Six to eight beads
Potpourri
Sewing thread

Beading:

Fill the box with potpourri. Place the box in the center of the napkin or handkerchief. Snugly tie opposite corners together in a knot. Repeat with remaining corners. This will create a Japanese knot.

Using the sewing thread, bead the corners of the napkin or handkerchief.

If necessary, refer to the photograph.

Materials for bag or pillow:

One sachet bag or
    one sachet pillow
An assortment of beads
Potpourri
Sewing thread

Beading:

Using the sewing thread, sew the beads to the sachet bag or sachet pillow.

Fill the sachet with potpourri.

If necessary, refer to the photograph.

pre-strung beaded candle shade

Materials:

One wire lamp shade form
Pre-strung glass beads
Industrial strength glue

Beading:

Starting at the top, glue the pre-strung beads around the lamp shade form.

The beads should be glued closely together as they are wrapped around the lamp shade form.

If necessary, refer to the photograph.

victorian candle shade

Materials:

One lamp shade
An assortment of beads
An assortment of silk flowers
Antique beaded glass fringe
Industrial strength glue

Beading:

Glue the silk flowers and the beads to the lamp shade, as desired.

Hand-sew the beaded fringe to the lower edge of the lamp shade.

If necessary, refer to the photograph.

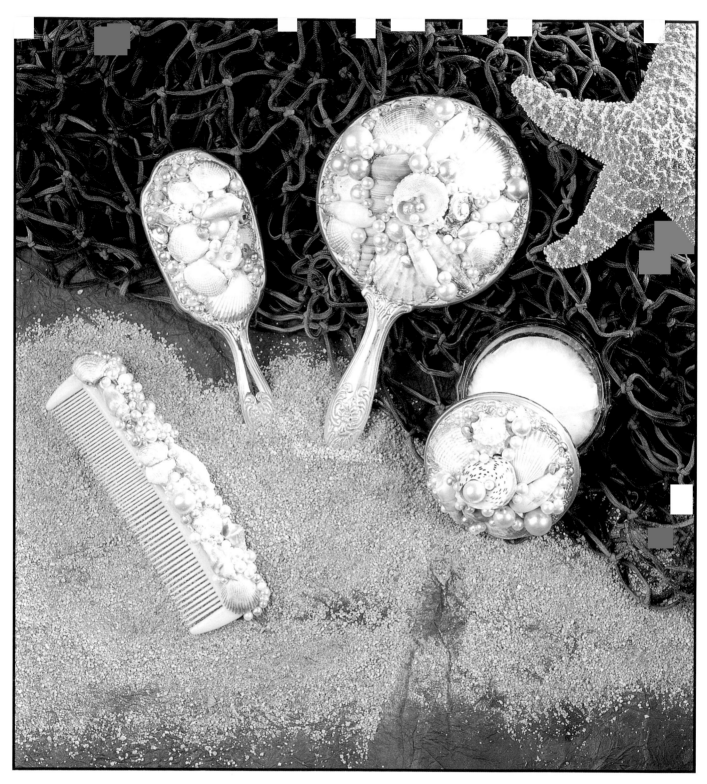

beaded
vanity set

Materials:

Vanity set —
  mirror, brush, comb,
  and poweder compact
An assortment of faux pearls
  in a variety of colors and sizes
An assortment of small shells
One silver paint marker
Industrial strength glue

Beading:

Using glue, embellish the
vanity set with the shells and the
faux pearls.

Using the silver paint marker,
color over the shells and the
faux pearls.

If necessary, refer to the
photograph.

icicles

Materials for one:

Gold thread
1/2 yard each of 4mm silk ribbons
Glass beads with large holes
3 1/2" soft-sculpture needle
Industrial strength glue

Beading:

Dip the needle in the glue. Slide on one bead and push it slightly past the eye of the needle. Dip the needle in the glue again and slide on another bead.

Take 1/2 yard of ribbon and slide it onto the needle 1/2" from one end of the ribbon. Fold the ribbon over, creating loops, and stick the needle through each fold. Slide it up to the bead. Continue to dip the needle in the glue and thread on the beads and ribbons.

Tie the gold thread around the top bead to act as a hanger.

flower vase

Materials:

One flower vase
Stained-glass window copper
   with self-adhesive tape
   on one side
An assortment of crystals
Beading thread or wire
Industrial strength glue

Beading:

Add crystals to the beading thread or wire to create "dangles." Glue these dangles to the top rim of the vase, spacing them evenly around the perimeter. Unpeel one inch of copper tape, and apply the tape around the top rim of the vase over the dangles. Secure the copper tape.

If necessary, refer to the photograph.

blue metal drawer knobs

Materials:

Metal drawer knobs
   with holes or loops
Blue acrylic paint
An assortment of beads,
   charms, or crystals
Several jump rings or wire

Beading:

   The number of drawer knobs needed will depend on the item to which you will be attaching them.

   Paint the metal drawer knobs, or leave them with their original finish.

   Using jump rings or wire, attach an assortment of beads, charms, or crystals to the holes or loops on the knobs. Follow the directions for embellishing simple objects found in the General Instructions on page 17.

   If necessary, refer to the photograph.

Drawer knobs can also be embellished with beads by simply gluing the beads onto them.

sun face knobs

Materials:

Round wooden drawer knobs
Gold-tone face charms
Acrylic paints:
    Navy blue
    Gold
    Metallic Gold
    White
Industrial strength glue
Clear gloss acrylic spray

Beading:

Paint the drawer knobs with navy blue acrylic paint.

Cut the loops off the charms if necessary and glue the charms to the drawer knobs in the bottom left hand corner.

At random, paint sun rays with gold and metallic gold acrylic paints coming out from the sun's face.

If desired, speckle the rays with white acrylic paint dots.

Let the paint dry thoroughly and spray with clear gloss acrylic spray.

If necessary, refer to the photograph.

golden egg

Materials:

One 2 3/4" craft paper egg
Gold acrylic paint
Fifteen freshwater pearls
Eighty blue #2 bugle beads
125 pink #2 bugle beads
155 green #2 bugle beads
Jump ring or split ring
Industrial strength glue

Beading:

Paint the craft paper egg with the gold acrylic paint. Measure around the egg, and divide the circumference into five equal sections. Mark the dividing points with a light pencil mark. The beads will be glued over the line later, so it will not show.

Begin the gluing on the row of pink bugle bead peaks, then add the blue and green rows. Decrease the number of beads in each row as you work from pink to green to accommodate the curve of the egg.

Add the floral patterns as shown in the diagram below.

It may help to draw the pattern on the egg before gluing on the beads.

If necessary, refer to the photograph.

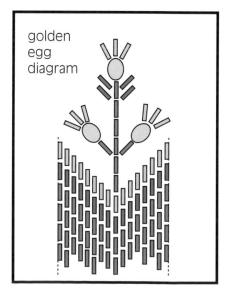

golden
egg
diagram

christmas egg

Materials:

One 2 3/4" craft paper egg
Sixty gold 15mm bugle beads
130 red 6/0 seed beads
200 gold #2 bugle beads
130 green #2 bugle beads
150 metallic green
    11/0 seed beads
Jump ring or split ring
Industrial strength glue

Beading:

Glue the band of 15mm bugle beads around the center of the egg, shifting the position of the beads as needed to make the pattern fit evenly.

Glue a band of red 6/0 seed beads and green #2 bugle beads above and below the center band. Outside each of these bands, glue on a row of metallic green 11/0 beads with the sides up so the holes are not visible.

Fill in the remainder of the upper and lower spaces with gold #2 bugle beads. Work in horizontal rows, decreasing the number of beads in each row to accommodate the curve of the egg.

If necessary, refer to the photograph.

heart ornament

Materials:

Dark red polymer clay
Dark red matte rainbow beads:
    Approximately 200
        11/0 seed beads
    Approximately thirty
        6/0 seed beads
    Approximately thirty
        #2 bugle beads
Small wire loop
Varnish, if desired

Beading:

Following the directions for working with polymer clay found in the General Instructions on page 18, condition the clay and roll it out in a thin layer.

Using the heart template, cut out the shape using a knife.

Following the diagram, press the beads into the surface of the clay.

After all the beads have been placed, trim away excess clay. Insert the wire loop for hanging and bake.

If necessary, refer to the photograph.

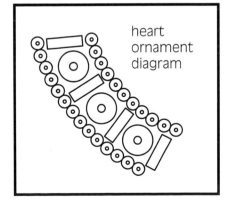

heart ornament diagram

heart ornament template

wooden tray

Materials:

One wooden tray
One piece of wrapping paper
An assortment of
   small rhinestones
Decoupage
Brush
Industrial strength glue

Beading:

Cut and arrange the wrapping paper on the wooden tray. Decoupage the wrapping paper onto the wooden tray following manufacturer's instructions. Let the decoupage dry thoroughly.

Using an assortment of small rhinestones, embellish the design on the wrapping paper by gluing them to the tray.

If necessary, refer to the photograph.

safety-pin basket

Materials:

Eighty-one size 1 safety pins,
 gold- or silver-tone finish
303 faceted crystal beads (8mm)
25-gauge gold wire
Needle-nose pliers

Beading:

Add two beads to each safety pin. To create the bottom of the basket, start by threading one safety pin (through the bottom hole) and one bead onto a piece of wire. Continue this pattern until 18 safety pins and 18 beads have been used.

After each layer, form the beaded length into a circle, and, using needle-nose pliers, twist the wire ends tightly together. Trim the ends. A new piece of wire is used for each layer.

The next layer will be threaded in the following order: one bead, one safety pin (through the top hole), one safety pin (through the bottom hole), one safety pin (through the top hole), and one bead. Refer to the diagram. Continue this pattern until nine new safety pins and nine beads have been used.

The third layer will be threaded in the following order: one bead, one safety pin (through the bottom hole), one safety pin (through the top hole), one safety pin (through the bottom hole), and one bead. Refer to the diagram. Continue this pattern until 18 new safety pins and nine beads have been used.

The top layer will be threaded in the same order as the third layer. Continue this pattern until 36 new safety pins and 18 beads have been used.

The top, scalloped row will be threaded in the following order: one bead, one safety pin (through the top hole), two

beads, and one safety pin (through the top hole). Continue this pattern until 54 beads have been used.

Shape the top of the basket. The handle is made from three loops, each made up of 11 beads.

Beading options:

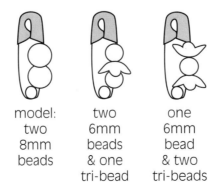

| model: two 8mm beads | two 6mm beads & one tri-bead | one 6mm bead & two tri-beads |

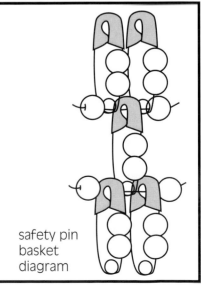

safety pin basket diagram

victorian ornaments

Materials for each ornament:

About ten grams of
    metallic gold 11/0 seed beads
About twenty grams of ivory or
    cream 11/0 seed beads
Sewing thread
4" x 4" piece of card stock
Photographic or painted image
    to fit in frame opening
10" length of narrow red ribbon
10" length of narrow
    green ribbon
3" circle of self-adhesive
    gold metallic paper
    for backing

Beading:

Following the directions for
surface beading found in the
General Instructions on page 19,
transfer the beading patterns
onto the card stock. Following
the diagrams, sew the beads
onto the card stock.

Using the templates, cut the
images to be mounted, and glue
them into the openings in the
center of the beadwork. Apply
the self-adhesive gold backing to
the backs of the beadwork, and
press carefully so all the threads
are in close contact with the gold
backing. Carefully trim away the
excess card and gold backing.

Form a loop and bow using
the red and green ribbons. Trim
the ends, and sew or glue the
bows to the center tops.

victorian ornaments templates (enlarge 142%)

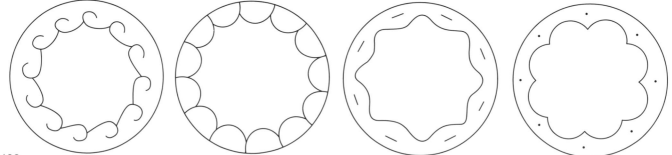

hanging wooden ornaments

Materials:

Wooden curtain finials
  in an assortment of
  sizes and shapes
Thick gold thread
One straight pin
Acrylic paint
Brushes
Pre-strung bugle beads
Pre-strung seed beads
Braid or tassels
Wood glue
Industrial strength glue

Beading:

Using wood glue, glue the wooden curtain finials together to construct an ornament.

Tie the thick gold thread into a loop, and push a straight pin through the thread into the top of the ornament. This will act as a hanger.

Paint the wooden ornament with acrylic paint. Let the paint dry completely.

Decorate the ornament by gluing on pre-strung beads. Braid or tassels can be added to the bottom of the ornament simply by gluing them in place.

If necessary, refer to the photograph.

embellished canning jar

Materials:

One canning jar
One decorator lid cover
Ten inches of lace
An assortment of beads,
   crystals, or charms
Beading thread

Beading:

Wrap the lace around the top of the canning-jar opening. Adjust to fit. Hand-sew the ends together, clipping off any excess lace.

Choosing a pattern, sew the beads onto the lower edge of the lace using beading thread. Continue all the way around the lace. The lace can be removed from the jar — this will make it easier to sew the beads onto the lace.

If necessary, refer to the photograph.

metal pot stand

Materials:

One miniature metal pot stand
An assortment of metal charms
An assortment of beads
Several jump rings or
　24-gauge wire
Miniature flowerpots
　to fit stand
Black acrylic paint
Silver acrylic paint

Beading:

Using jump rings or wire, randomly attach the metal charms and beads to the metal pot stand.

Paint the flowerpots to match the color of the pot stand.

If necessary, refer to the photograph.

bronze candlestick collar

Materials:

One ounce of bronze metallic
    11/0 seed beads
Eight bronze 8mm
    faceted crystals
One beading needle
Sewing thread to match beads

Beading:

Thread the beading needle with a double strand of thread. Knot the thread at one end. Slip one bronze metallic 11/0 seed bead onto the thread, and bring it to 2 inches from the knot, then run the needle back through the bead. Add 59 more beads onto the thread. Run the needle back through the beads to form a closed loop.

Add loops around the closed loop. Each of the 12 loops are made from 11 beads.

Add the triangle-shaped sections, placing the crystals where indicated. When all four triangles are complete, bury the thread in the work until it is secure, then clip close. Refer to the diagram below.

If necessary, refer to the photograph.

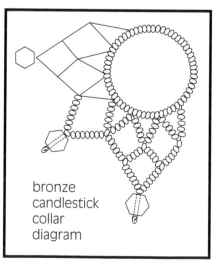

bronze
candlestick
collar
diagram

crystal candlestick skirt

Materials:

One white plastic drapery ring,
    1 1/2" diameter
Beads for each drop:
    One white with AB finish
        6mm faceted
        firepolish crystal
    Nine crystal rainbow
        6/0 seed beads
    Two silver-lined crystal
        15mm bugle beads
    Forty-eight crystal rainbow
        11/0 seed beads
One beading needle
White sewing thread

Beading:

As shown in the diagram below, attach the knotted thread to the plastic drapery ring. Attach at least 12, but no more than 20 drops.

When necessary, add a new thread by tying a square knot. Finish the last drop, then secure the thread by looping it into the beads on the first drop. Bury the thread in the beads of the first drop and clip close.

If necessary, refer to the photograph.

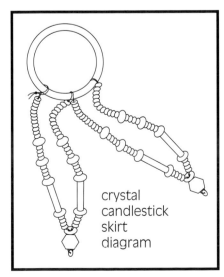

crystal
candlestick
skirt
diagram

gourd ornament

Materials:

One hollow gourd with a
   hole drilled in the bottom
One tassel
Cream acrylic paint
Gold acrylic paint
Leaf charms
Eight to 10 large beads
Eighteen inches of
   matching cord
Glue gun and glue sticks

Beading:

Paint the gourd with the cream acrylic paint. Let the paint dry completely. Wash the gourd with the gold acrylic paint. Let the paint dry completely.

Using a glue gun, glue the tassel into the hole in the bottom of the gourd. Glue the leaf charms and the beads to the top of the gourd. Attach the cord for hanging.

If necessary, refer to the photograph.

metric conversions ...

INCHES TO MILLIMETRES AND CENTIMETRES

MM-Millimetres   CM-Centimetres

INCHES	MM	CM	INCHES	CM	INCHES	CM
$1/8$	3	0.9	9	22.9	30	76.2
$1/4$	6	0.6	10	25.4	31	78.7
$3/8$	10	1.0	11	27.9	32	81.3
$1/2$	13	1.3	12	30.5	33	83.8
$5/8$	16	1.6	13	33.0	34	86.4
$3/4$	19	1.9	14	35.6	35	88.9
$7/8$	22	2.2	15	38.1	36	91.4
1	25	2.5	16	40.6	37	94.0
$1 1/4$	32	3.2	17	43.2	38	96.5
$1 1/2$	38	3.8	18	45.7	39	99.1
$1 3/4$	44	4.4	19	48.3	40	101.6
2	51	5.1	20	50.8	41	104.1
$2 1/2$	64	6.4	21	53.3	42	106.7
3	76	7.6	22	55.9	43	109.2
$3 1/2$	89	8.9	23	58.4	44	111.8
4	102	10.2	24	61.0	45	114.3
$4 1/2$	114	11.4	25	63.5	46	116.8
5	127	12.7	26	66.0	47	119.4
6	152	15.2	27	68.6	48	121.9
7	178	17.8	28	71.1	49	124.5
8	203	20.3	29	73.7	50	127.0

YARDS TO METRES

YARDS	METRES	YARDS	METRES	YARDS	METRES	YARDS	METRES	YARDS	METRES
$1/8$	0.11	$2 1/8$	1.94	$4 1/8$	3.77	$6 1/8$	5.60	$8 1/8$	7.43
$1/4$	0.23	$2 1/4$	2.06	$4 1/4$	3.89	$6 1/4$	5.72	$8 1/4$	7.54
$3/8$	0.34	$2 3/8$	2.17	$4 3/8$	4.00	$6 3/8$	5.83	$8 3/8$	7.66
$1/2$	0.46	$2 1/2$	2.29	$4 1/2$	4.11	$6 1/2$	5.94	$8 1/2$	7.77
$5/8$	0.57	$2 5/8$	2.40	$4 5/8$	4.23	$6 5/8$	6.06	$8 5/8$	7.89
$3/4$	0.69	$2 3/4$	2.51	$4 3/4$	4.34	$6 3/4$	6.17	$8 3/4$	8.00
$7/8$	0.80	$2 7/8$	2.63	$4 7/8$	4.46	$6 7/8$	6.29	$8 7/8$	8.12
1	0.91	3	2.74	5	4.57	7	6.40	9	8.23
$1 1/8$	1.03	$3 1/8$	2.86	$5 1/8$	4.69	$7 1/8$	6.52	$9 1/8$	8.34
$1 1/4$	1.14	$3 1/4$	2.97	$5 1/4$	4.80	$7 1/4$	6.63	$9 1/4$	8.46
$1 3/8$	1.26	$3 3/8$	3.09	$5 3/8$	4.91	$7 3/8$	6.74	$9 3/8$	8.57
$1 1/2$	1.37	$3 1/2$	3.20	$5 1/2$	5.03	$7 1/2$	6.86	$9 1/2$	8.69
$1 5/8$	1.49	$3 5/8$	3.31	$5 5/8$	5.14	$7 5/8$	6.97	$9 5/8$	8.80
$1 3/4$	1.60	$3 3/4$	3.43	$5 3/4$	5.26	$7 3/4$	7.09	$9 3/4$	8.92
$1 7/8$	1.71	$3 7/8$	3.54	$5 7/8$	5.37	$7 7/8$	7.20	$9 7/8$	9.03
2	1.83	4	3.66	6	5.49	8	7.32	10	9.14

index ...

A little about beads, 10-11
Adding a new length
    of thread, 16, 17, 18
Amber & cloisonne necklace, 23
Amber & jade pin, 64-65
Amethyst cabochon earrings, 43
Anklets, 61
Artistic dangle earrings, 52-53
Assembling
    beaded connectors, 16
Attaching clasps, 16
Attaching end caps, 16
Aztec frame, 100
Backtracking, 19
Bargello barrette, 71
Barrettes, 71-75
Basket, 119
Bead shapes, 9
Bead sizes, 12
Beaded collar & pockets, 86
Beaded connectors, 14, 16
Beaded hairsticks, 78
Beaded pear necklace, 32
Beaded strawberry necklace, 32
Beaded vanity set, 112
Beading components, 13
Beehive stationery box &
    note cards, 97
Bezel cups, 13
Black lace collar, 82
Blazer cuffs & pocket, 87
Blue diamond barrette, 72
Blue metal drawer knobs, 114
Blue on blue necklace, 33
Bottles, 94-95
Bracelets, 37, 40, 55-60
Braided bracelet, 55
Brick-stitching, 17
Bronze & iris
    crystal necklace, 26-27
Bronze candlestick collar, 124
Bugle beads, 9, 19
Butterfly stationery box, 97
Button bracelet, 56
Button cover blanks, 13
Button covers, 90-91
Cabochon &
    crystal votive cup, 103
Cabochon &
    pearls bracelet, 58-59
Cabochon bracelets, 58-59
Cabochons, 9, 12
Candelabra, 108
Candle shades, 110-111
Candles, 107
Candlesticks, 124-125
Celtic weave combs, 76
Ceramic beads, 11
Charm bottles, 95
Cherub frame, 101
Chevron necklace, 28-29
Christmas egg, 116
Cinnabar stick pin, 68
Clasps, 14, 16
Clay beads, 11
Clear crystal napkin rings, 106
Clinch combs, 77
Coil necklace, 31
Coin dress, 88
Collars, 81-82, 86
Combs, 76-77
Component earrings, 50-51
Copal hairsticks, 79
Coral anklet, 61

Cosmic leather pin, 64
Couching, 19
Crimping, 17, 19
Crimps, 15, 17, 19
Crystal candlestick skirt, 125
Crystal-drop candelabra, 108
Crystal necklaces, 26-27
Crystal swirl necklace, 26-27
Cuffs, 87
Daisy pin, 66-67
Dangle charm pin, 65
Dangle hairsticks, 79
Decor, 92-126
Decorative eggs, 116
Drawer knobs, 114-115
Dress, 88
Ear cuffs, 54
Ear findings, 13
Earrings, 36-53
Embellished canning jar, 122
Embellished lace necklace, 35
Embellishing simple objects, 17
Embellishments, 83-84
Emerald hairsticks, 79
End caps, 15, 16
End cups, 15
Expansion bracelet, 57
Eyepins, 14
Faceted beads, 9
Fancy shaped beads, 9
Figure-eight connectors, 14
Findings & components, 14-15
Finishing strands, 17
Flat disk button covers, 91
Floral barrettes, 74
Floral oval pin, 62
Flower vase, 102, 113
Frames, 100-101
French wire, 13
French wire earrings, 46
Frosted amber
    pocket embellishment, 83
Frosted votive cups, 103
Fusing fabric, 17
General instructions, 16-19
Glass beads, 10
Gloves, 89
Golden egg, 116
Gourd ornament, 126
Green yipes stripes necklace,
    bracelet & earrings, 37
Hair, 70-79
Hairsticks, 78-79
Hanging wooden ornaments, 121
Headpins, 14
Heart ornament, 117
Hex earrings, 48-49
House magnet, 96
Icicles, 113
Indian agate bracelet, 58-59
Indian agate necklace
    & earrings, 39
Jade tree in clay pot, 98-99
Jeweled heart boxes, 93
Jewelry, 20-69
Jingle bells necklace
    & earrings, 41
Large round bead napkin rings, 106
Lavender matte necklace, 30
Lilac tassel necklace
    & earrings, 38
Liquid silver anklet, 61
Liquid silver bracelet, 60
Lucky elephant necklace, 24-25
Metal beads, 10
Metal pot stand, 123
Metric conversions, 127
Multi-bracelet bracelet, 57

Multi-color button covers, 90
Napkin rings, 106
Natural beads, 11
Necklaces, 21-41
Needle-weaving, 18
Ornaments, 117, 120, 121, 126
Oval flower pin, 62-63
Pansy pin, 66-67
Pastel braided bracelet, 55
Pastel crystal necklace, 26
Pearl & lace collar, 81
Pearl anklet, 61
Pearl spray earrings, 42
Perfume bottles, 94
Peruvian bracelet, 56
Petit flower pins, 66-67
Petite paisley pin, 62-63
Pin backs, 13
Pins, 62-67
Plastic beads, 10
Pockets, 83-87
Polymer clay earrings, 47
Porcelain rose necklace, 34
Posy pin, 66-67
Pressing beads into clay, 18
Pre-strung beaded candle shade, 110-111
Pre-strung beads, 13
Purple diamond barrette, 73
Random twist necklaces, 21-22
Rings, 15
Rosary beads, 69
Round beads, 9, 12
Sachet box, bag & pillow, 109
Safety-pin basket, 119
Sand dollar earrings, 45
Seed beads, 9, 19
Sets, 36-41
Seven cabochon bracelet, 58-59
Silver & amethyst
    cabochon watch, 59
Silver heart earrings, 44
Simple garment embellishments, 84-85
Square knot, 29
Stationery boxes, 97
Stick pins, 68
Striped clay necklace
    & earrings, 36
Suncatchers, 104-105
Sun face knobs, 115
Sun-star earrings, 45
Surface beading, 19
Three-drop stick pin, 68
Tools, 12
Tortoise shell barrette, 75
Triple rainbow necklace, 31
Tulip pin, 66-67
Turquoise cabochon earrings, 44
Turquoise drop earrings, 42
Turquoise drum necklace, 24-25
Turquoise hairsticks, 79
Turquoise tube necklace, 24
Twisted bracelet, 60
Vanity set, 112
Vases, 102, 113
Velvet rose ribbon barrette, 75
Victorian candle shade, 111
Victorian ornaments, 120
Votive cups, 103, 113
Watch, 59
Wearables, 80-91
White disk bracelet, 56
Wooden tray, 118
Working with leather cord, 19
Working with polymer clay, 18
Yin-yang necklace,
    bracelet & earrings, 40
Zuni bear earrings, 43